The Times-Picayune

SUPER
SAINTS

A salute to the 2010 Super Bowl champions

The Times-Picayune

Designed by Adrianna Garcia and Beth McCoy
Edited by Michael J. Montalbano and Trey Iles
Photo editing by Doug Parker

PHOTOGRAPHERS Chuck Cook, Rusty Costanza, Michael DeMocker, Brett Duke, Chris Granger, David Grunfeld, Matthew Hinton, Ted Jackson, Eliot Kamenitz, John McCusker, Susan Poag, Scott Threlkeld
CONTRIBUTING WRITERS John DeShazier, Jeff Duncan, Peter Finney, Nakia Hogan, Mike Triplett, Brian Allee-Walsh, Ed Anderson, Mary Sparacello
SPORTS EDITOR Doug Tatum
DESIGN DIRECTOR George Berke
ASSISTANT PHOTO EDITORS G. Andrew Boyd, David Grunfeld, Dinah Rogers
PHOTO IMAGING Matthew Hinton

Dan Shea, Managing Editor/News

978-0-9844542-1-1
Cover photos by Michael DeMocker

CONTENTS

GAME 1: SAINTS VS. LIONS 6

GAME 2: SAINTS AT EAGLES 12

QUARTERBACK DREW BREES 18

GAME 3: SAINTS AT BILLS 22

GAME 4: SAINTS VS. JETS 28

GAME 5: SAINTS VS. GIANTS 34

GAME 6: SAINTS AT DOLPHINS 40

GAME 7: SAINTS VS. FALCONS 48

GAME 8: SAINTS VS. PANTHERS 54

GAME 9: SAINTS AT RAMS 60

GAME 10: SAINTS AT BUCCANEERS 64

GAME 11: SAINTS VS. PATRIOTS 70

GAME 12: SAINTS AT REDSKINS 80

FANTASTIC FANS 86

GAME 13: SAINTS AT FALCONS 88

OWNER TOM BENSON 94

GAME 14: SAINTS VS. COWBOYS 98

GAME 15: SAINTS VS. BUCCANEERS 106

GAME 16: SAINTS AT PANTHERS 112

COACH SEAN PAYTON 118

NFC DIVISIONAL PLAYOFF GAME: SAINTS VS. CARDINALS 122

SAFETY DARREN SHARPER 130

NFC CHAMPIONSHIP GAME: SAINTS VS. VIKINGS 132

WHO DAT CONTROVERSY 142

DRESSING THE PART 142

ARRIVING IN MIAMI 143

SUPER BOWL XLIV: SAINTS VS. COLTS 144

NFL FINAL STANDINGS 156

SAINTS STATISTICS 157

ROSTER 158

MILESTONES, RECORDS 159

THROUGH THE YEARS 160

After New Orleans rained past Indianapolis 31-17 in Super Bowl XLIV at Sun Life Stadium in Miami on Feb. 7, 2010, the party kicks into high gear for Saints fans — with Bourbon Street a popular setting to celebrate the team's first NFL championship.

BRETT DUKE / THE TIMES-PICAYUNE

INTRODUCTION

On a stifling September day in 1967, John Gilliam returned the first kickoff in New Orleans Saints history 94-yards for a touchdown to the roaring approval of 80,879 fans at Tulane Stadium.

It was an auspicious beginning to a franchise that has known far more downs than ups in the intervening 43 years.

Sundays of frustration and heartache, of bag heads and Aints, of good teams producing playoff losses did not weaken the bonds between a feisty city and a struggling franchise.

Even Katrina, which chased the team from the Superdome and led to angry worries that the Saints would try to bolt forever, instead signaled a new beginning.

A new head coach in Sean Payton. A new quarterback in Drew Brees. A sold-out season. And in 2006, the team's first try for the NFC championship. The pieces of an elite team were finally coming together.

But it was a 40-yard field goal from the right hash mark of the Superdome in the NFC championship against the Vikings on Jan. 24, 2010, that gave the fans what they always dreamed for: a spot in the Super Bowl.

And for a city that thought it couldn't get any better, Drew Brees' dominating performance over the Colts brought a long-suffering city its first NFL championship.

Take a bow, Saints.

Take a bow, Who Dat fans.

SAINTS | LIONS

45 | **27**

Running back Mike Bell and the Saints' offense find success against the Lions, who were 0-16 last year, in the season opener.

DAVID GRUNFELD / THE TIMES-PICAYUNE

Safety Darren Sharper foils
Detroit rookie quarterback
Matthew Stafford once
again, snagging his second
interception of the game.

ELIOT KAMENITZ / THE TIMES-PICAYUNE

SAINTS | LIONS
45   27

AN UNEVEN START

The Saints' season-opening win and the standout efforts of quarterback Drew Brees are marred by mistakes

By Mike Triplett Staff writer

The Saints' 2009 debut was spectacular if it weren't so darn sloppy.

Their 45-27 victory over the Detroit Lions was a thing of beauty if it hadn't turned so ugly on a handful of occasions.

It was perfect if . . . well, come to think of it, it was. A perfect example of everything these Saints were capable of — good and bad — and a 1-0 start to a season that promised to be a thrill ride.

"We got a win; we scored a lot of points, but we could have scored a whole lot more," said fullback Heath Evans, who caught the last of quarterback Drew Brees' six touchdown passes — a career high for the prolific quarterback, who matched Billy Kilmer's 40-year-old franchise record.

Saints Coach Sean Payton said he told his team that he was "excited for the win" but frustrated by all the things "we did in this game to get you beat."

Brees was outstanding, throwing for 358 yards and connecting with five receivers for touchdowns. But he threw one interception when he tried to force a deep ball on a flea-flicker in the second quarter.

Running back Mike Bell also was terrific, for the most part. He rushed for a career-high 143 yards on 28 carries, but his fumble in the third quarter was returned 65 yards for a touchdown by Detroit.

The Saints snagged three interceptions from rookie quarterback Matthew Stafford — two by safety Darren Sharper — while slamming the door on the Lions' run game. The only real drawback was a 64-yard pass completion from Stafford to receiver Calvin Johnson in the third quarter that accounted for more than one-fourth of Detroit's 231 yards.

And the Saints struggled on special teams, with Reggie Bush's muffed punt in the second quarter, John Carney's blocked field-goal attempt and a handful of lengthy kick returns by Detroit keeping the game much closer than it was.

LIONS	1ST **3**	2ND **7**	3RD **17**	4TH **0**	F **27**
SAINTS	**14**	**14**	**10**	**7**	**45**

1-0

RECORD AFTER GAME 1

SCORING SUMMARY

1ST **SAINTS:** Marques Colston 9-yard pass from Drew Brees (John Carney kick). Five plays, 54 yards in 2:49.
SAINTS: Robert Meachem 39-yard pass from Brees (Carney kick). Three plays, 53 yards in 1:09.
LIONS: Jason Hanson 47-yard field goal. Nine plays, 51 yards in 4:22.

2ND **LIONS:** Kevin Smith 4-yard run (Hanson kick). Four plays, 13 yards in 2:05.
SAINTS: Jeremy Shockey 1-yard pass from Brees (Carney kick). Ten plays, 65 yards in 5:04.
SAINTS: Shockey 15-yard pass from Brees (Carney kick). Four plays, 59 yards in 1:11.

3RD **LIONS:** Matthew Stafford 1-yard run (Hanson kick). Eight plays, 71 yards in 3:13.
SAINTS: Carney 39-yard field goal. Ten plays, 64 yards in 5:36.
LIONS: Hanson 24-yard field goal. Six plays, 6 yards in 2:49.
SAINTS: Devery Henderson 58-yard pass from Brees (Carney kick). One play, 58 yards in 19 seconds.
LIONS: Louis Delmas 65-yard fumble return (Hanson kick).

4TH **SAINTS**: Heath Evans 13-yard pass from Brees (Carney kick). Thirteen plays, 78 yards in 8:00.

TEAM STATISTICS

	SAINTS	LIONS
FIRST DOWNS	**28**	**14**
TOTAL OFFENSIVE PLAYS-YARDS (NET)	**69-515**	**58-231**
RUSHES-YARDS (NET)	**35-157**	**20-33**
PASSING YARDS (NET)	**358**	**198**
PASSES (COMP-ATT-INT)	**26-34-1**	**16-37-3**
PUNTS (NUMBER-AVG)	**2-48.0**	**5-41.6**
PUNT RETURNS-YARDS	**3-11**	**2-55**
KICKOFF RETURNS-YARDS	**6-148**	**5-180**
PENALTY YARDS	**7-36**	**8-80**
FUMBLES-LOST	**3-2**	**0-0**
TIME OF POSSESSION	**36:30**	**23:30**
FIELD GOALS (ATT-MADE)	**2-1**	**2-2**

INDIVIDUAL STATISTICS

RUSHING
SAINTS: Mike Bell 28-143, Reggie Bush 7-14.
LIONS: Kevin Smith 15-29, Aaron Brown 1-9.

CHUCK COOK / THE TIMES-PICAYUNE

New Orleans' Mike Bell gets New Orleans off to a quick start, rushing for 143 yards on 28 carries against Detroit.

PASSING
SAINTS: Drew Brees 26-34-358-6-1.
LIONS: Matthew Stafford 16-37-205-0-3.

RECEIVING
SAINTS: Devery Henderson 5-103, Reggie Bush 5-55.
LIONS: Calvin Johnson 3-90, Kevin Smith 7-52.

INTERCEPTIONS
SAINTS: Darren Sharper 2, Scott Shanle 1.
LIONS: Anthony Henry 1.

SACKS
SAINTS: Jonathan Vilma 1.
LIONS: none.

TACKLES (unassisted)
SAINTS: Tracy Porter 6, Scott Fujita 5.
LIONS: Larry Foote 9, Anthony Henry 9.

DAVID GRUNFELD / THE TIMES-PICAYUNE

Saints quarterback Drew Brees kept the Lions at arms length all game, completing 26 of 34 passes for 358 yards, with six touchdowns (matching the franchise record) and one interception.

"We scored 45, and you look at it and we turned the ball over three times. We got a field goal blocked. There were a lot more opportunities out there to be had," Brees said. "That's a good thing, but then you realize it only gets tougher as we go along.

"We have a huge challenge next week at Philadelphia. They won today at Carolina, so we know we have our work cut out for us — and we're going to have to be better next week."

For a while, this game looked like it would turn into a laugher.

After Robert Meachem returned the opening kickoff 42 yards, the Saints needed five plays to score — on a 9-yard pass from Brees to Marques Colston.

The Saints' defense then forced a three-and-out, and the offense needed three plays to score its next touchdown — on a 39-yard pass from Brees to Meachem.

The score was 14-0 less than six minutes into the first quarter.

"We talked about that, starting the season off fast, and obviously this game," Brees said. "But, unfortunately, we kind of let them back in it."

Detroit cut the deficit to 14-10, thanks to some stalled drives by the Saints and a 43-yard punt return by Dennis Northcutt that set up a 4-yard touchdown run by tailback Kevin Smith on fourth-and-1 early in the second quarter.

The Saints then ran away again, with back-to-back touchdown passes from Brees to tight end Jeremy Shockey for a 28-10 lead with 1:10 remaining in the first half.

But New Orleans continued to leave the door open with a series of mishaps.

Bush muffed a punt in the final minute before halftime, giving the Lions the ball at the Saints' 15-yard line.

"I can't really put my finger on it, but whatever it is, it can't happen again," said Bush, who fumbled two punt returns but recovered the other one.

Bush had a rough day, gaining 55 yards on five receptions but running for just 14 yards on seven carries. He refused to blame the time he missed during the preseason with a bruised calf, saying there was "no excuse" for the way he played.

Sharper bailed Bush out when he intercepted a pass on the Lions' next play, and he returned it 51 yards and into Detroit territory. But the Saints failed to capitalize when Carney's 34-yard field-goal attempt was blocked.

"We can be very dangerous, but we still can't beat ourselves," New Orleans defensive end Will Smith said. "The Lions were a pretty good team, but we were a little bit better today. And you know, next week we may be playing a better team — and we have to be even better than we played this week and play mistake-free."

SAINTS | EAGLES

48   22

The Saints' Jeremy Shockey and
Marques Colston (12) celebrate after
Colston caught a 25-yard touchdown
pass in the second quarter.

CHUCK COOK / THE TIMES-PICAYUNE

13

SAINTS | EAGLES

48   **22**

UP, UP & AWAY

New Orleans' offense, defense and special teams all rise to the challenge with Philadelphia left in the dust

By Brian Allee-Walsh Staff writer

Losing five close games during an 8-8 campaign in 2008 left an indelible impression on Saints Coach Sean Payton, his staff and players. In fact, it spawned a T-shirt in training camp bearing a simple six-letter word to remind them of a road they didn't want to go down again.

The T-shirt carried the Super XLIV logo and read: "Finish."

Before a sellout crowd of 69,144 at Lincoln Financial Field in Philadelphia, the Saints practiced what they had preached the past nine months.

New Orleans finished off Philadelphia in impressive fashion, outscoring the Eagles 31-9 in the second half and coasted to a 48-22 victory to establish itself as a legitimate player in the talent-rich NFC.

Veteran Saints free safety Darren Sharper sealed the deal with 55 seconds remaining, returning his third interception of the young season 97 yards for a touchdown.

By then, it didn't matter. Thousands of stunned Eagles fans had flown the coop, wondering perhaps what might have been if injured quarterback Donovan McNabb had played instead of backup Kevin Kolb.

New Orleans quarterback Drew Brees continued his early mastery, completing 25 of 34 passes for 311 yards and three touchdowns, including 15 and 25 yarders to wide receiver Marques Colston. Running back Mike Bell imposed his will before leaving with a sprained right knee in the fourth quarter, rushing 17 times for 86 yards and one touchdown.

The Saints' defense and special teams also came up with four turnovers, resulting in the Eagles' second-most lopsided defeat at "The Linc," eclipsed only by a 42-0 loss to the Seattle Seahawks in Week 13 of the 2005 season.

"We want to have the mentality that if we have a team down, we want to stomp on their throat and not let them come back," Sharper said.

Said Saints middle linebacker Jonathan Vilma: "Losing the way we did last season, we felt like we had to

SUPER SAINTS

New Orleans' Mike Bell gets some hang time on a 7-yard touchdown run in the third quarter.
CHUCK COOK / THE TIMES-PICAYUNE

| EAGLES | 1ST 7 | 2ND 6 | 3RD 7 | 4TH 2 | F 22 |
| SAINTS | 10 | 7 | 17 | 14 | 48 |

"We want to
have the
mentality that
if we have a
team down,
we want to
stomp on
their throat
and not let
them come
back."
DARREN SHARPER

2-0

RECORD AFTER GAME 2

INDIVIDUAL STATISTICS

SAINTS: Mike Bell 17-86, Reggie Bush 10-33.
EAGLES: Brian Wesbrook 13-52, LeSean McCoy 5-18.

PASSING

SAINTS: Drew Brees 25-34-311-3-1.
EAGLES: Kevin Kolb 31-51-391-2-3.

RECEIVING

SAINTS: Marques Colston 8-98, Jeremy Shockey 4-49.
EAGLES: Brent Celek 8-104, Jason Avant 7-79.

INTERCEPTIONS

SAINTS: Tracy Porter 1, Scott Shanle 1, Darren Sharper 1.
EAGLES: Akeem Jordan 1.

SACKS

SAINTS: Roman Harper 1, Bobby McCray 1.
EAGLES: Trent Cole 1, Juqua Parker 1.

TACKLES (unassisted)

SAINTS: Scott Shanle 10, Roman Harper 7.
EAGLES: Quintin Mikell 10, Akeem Jordan 7.

CHUCK COOK / THE TIMES-PICAYUNE
New Orleans safety Darren Sharper returns an interception 97 yards for a touchdown in the fourth quarter.

SUPER SAINTS

GAME STATISTICS
Attendance: 69,144 at Lincoln Financial Field

SCORING SUMMARY

1ST
SAINTS: Marques Colston 15-yard pass from Drew Brees (John Carney kick). Eight plays, 74 yards in 4:06.
EAGLES: DeSean Jackson 71-yard pass from Kevin Kolb (David Akers kick). Four plays, 85 yards in 1:51.
SAINTS: Carney 23-yard field goal. Ten plays, 48 yards in 3:21.

2ND
EAGLES: Akers 23-yard field goal. Fifteen plays, 68 yards in 8:20.
SAINTS: Colston 25-yard pass from Brees (John Carney kick). Two plays, 54 yards in 37 seconds.
EAGLES: Akers 32-yard field goal. Seven plays, 65 yards in 43 seconds.

3RD
SAINTS: Heath Evans 11-yard pass from Brees (Carney kick). Three plays, 22 yards in 1:10.
SAINTS: Mike Bell 7-yard run (Carney kick). Four plays, 24 yards in 1:19.
SAINTS: Carney 25-yard field goal. Twelve plays, 70 yards in 6:16.
EAGLES: Jason Avant 3-yard pass from Kolb (Akers kick). Eight plays, 35 yards in 3:41.

4TH
SAINTS: Reggie Bush 19-yard run (Carney kick). Six plays, 52 yards in 3:14.
EAGLES: Brees fumbled out of bounds in the end zone for a safety.
SAINTS: Darren Sharper 97-yard interception return (Carney kick).

TEAM STATISTICS

	SAINTS	EAGLES
FIRST DOWNS	23	23
TOTAL OFFENSIVE PLAYS-YARDS (NET)	65-421	75-463
RUSHES-YARDS (NET)	29-133	21-85
PASSING YARDS (NET)	288	378
PASSES (COMP-ATT-INT)	25-34-1	31-52-3
PUNTS (NUMBER-AVG)	3-52.0	5-45.0
PUNT RETURNS-YARDS	2-3	2-5
KICKOFF RETURNS-YARDS	3-72	8-186
PENALTY YARDS	3-13	7-45
FUMBLES-LOST	2-0	1-1
TIME OF POSSESSION	30:26	29:34
FIELD GOALS (ATT-MADE)	2-2	2-2

CHUCK COOK / THE TIMES-PICAYUNE
The Saints' Marques Colston hauls in a 15-yard touchdown pass in the first quarter.

come up with something that is pertinent to our team, especially after last year. When you're 0-5 in games that were decided by one, two, three points, we definitely have to finish games this season. We have to recognize it, understand it and do it.

"Today, we did that. Hopefully, there'll be more to come."

New Orleans rode the momentum of a six-minute stretch at the end of the first half and the start of the second to its second victory in as many games.

From the 2:38 mark of the second quarter to 11:39 left in the third quarter, the Saints outscored the Eagles 21-3 to break away from a 10-10 tie and seize control at 31-13.

The Saints' special teams keyed the flurry, thanks in part to a poor decision by Eagles punt returner DeSean Jackson, questionable clock management by Philadelphia Coach Andy Reid and a turnover by Eagles kick returner Ellis Hobbs.

With the score tied at 10 inside the two-minute warning, Jackson elected to field a 60-yard punt by Thomas Morstead inside the Eagles' 5-yard line. A penalty negated Jackson's 31-yard return, giving Philadelphia horrible field position at its 3-yard line.

Questionable play calling and a dropped pass on third down by Jackson enabled New Orleans to take over at its 46 with 1:20 remaining. A 29-yard pass from Brees to

Reggie Bush put the ball at the Eagles' 25. On the next play, Brees and Colston hooked up for a touchdown and a 17-10 lead with 43 seconds remaining.

But David Akers' 23-yard field goal as time expired trimmed the Saints' lead to 17-13 at halftime.

The death knell sounded for the Eagles on the second-half kickoff when Saints cornerback Malcolm Jenkins stripped the ball from Hobbs, and safety Chris Reis recovered at Philadelphia's 22.

Two plays later, Brees connected with fullback Heath Evans on an 11-yard touchdown pass. Evans broke two tackles and somehow stayed in bounds to stretch the ball inside the right pylon for his second touchdown in as many games.

"Drew said early on during OTAs that we want to make sure that we want to finish strong," Sharper said. "You got to win close games if you want to be a championship team, and we have the mentality that we want to be a championship team.

"We didn't make any statement today. It was a great victory on the road against a quality NFC opponent, but statements this early in the season are overrated. Sure, people are going to be talking about us right now, but we can't worry about that too much. We still have a lot of football left."

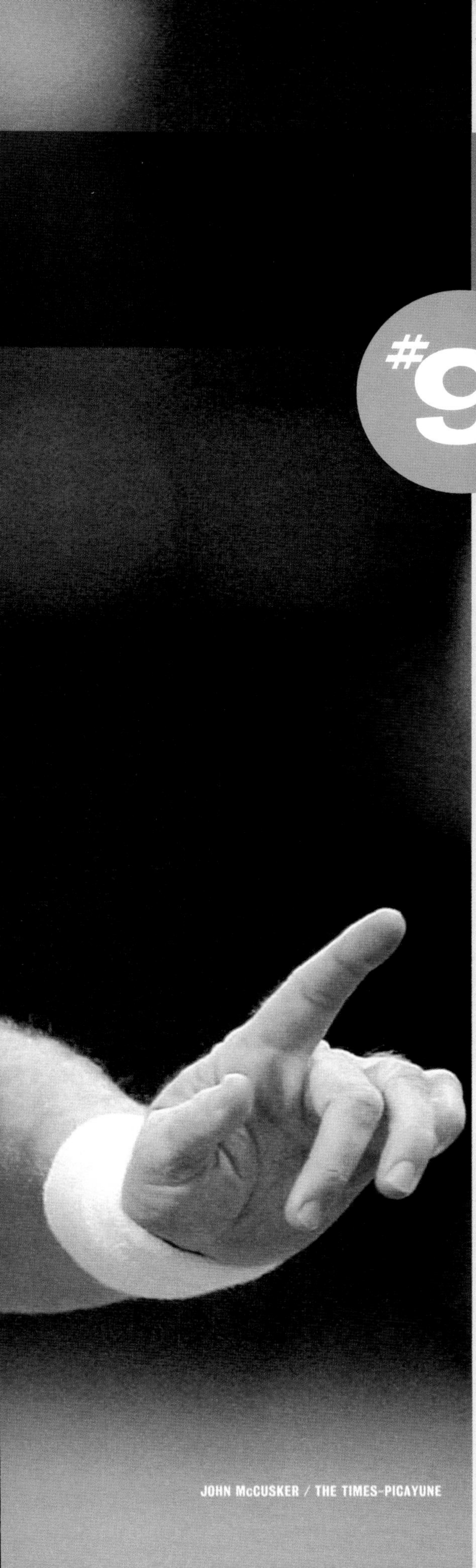

DREW BREES

#9

Once down and out, Drew Brees and New Orleans now shine like never before after the two join forces

By Mike Triplett Staff writer

Saints quarterback Drew Brees had built a strong enough relationship with the city of New Orleans that he finally admitted it: He was leaning toward signing with the Miami Dolphins in 2006 when the NFL teams competed for his services during free agency.

From a football perspective, it was a no-brainer. The Saints had just finished a 3-13 season and were starting over with new coach Sean Payton. The Dolphins, meanwhile, had rebuilt themselves under former LSU coach Nick Saban, coming off a 9-7 season.

"And just looking at it from an outsider's perspective, not knowing anything about New Orleans other than Mardi Gras, you're thinking, 'New Orleans vs. Miami,'" said Brees, Miami rolling off his tongue like a game-show host announcing the grand prize. "And I'm coming from San Diego, where Miami would be less of a transition. So naturally going into it, I was leaning toward Miami."

New Orleans, on the other hand, was in transition. About six months earlier, the city was devastated by Hurricane Katrina, leaving its future and that of its NFL franchise in doubt.

But all of Brees' concerns were quashed after one aggressive recruiting trip in which he visited Saints officials. After visiting the team's brass, he felt as if he had found a place where he belonged.

During the 2009 season, Brees took a break from the playing field when he and his wife, Brittany, attended the dedication of the Brees Family Field at Lusher Charter School, which was renovated using money from the Brees Dream Foundation and Operation Kids.

It was one of 12 projects throughout New Orleans aided by Brees' charitable foundation, which had raised $1.8 million.

The NFL recognized Brees for his various good works,

QUARTERBACK

DREW BREES

selecting him its Man of the Year after his first season with the Saints. He shared the honor with former Chargers teammate LaDainian Tomlinson for their contributions on and off the field.

"This is where I belong, and I felt like this was a calling," Brees said.

The Saints admitted something, too.

They got lucky when Brees went down with a torn labrum and damaged rotator cuff in his right throwing arm during the final game of the 2005 season. The injury and subsequent recovery time scared off almost every team in the NFL during free agency two months later.

Brees' former team, the Chargers, showed tepid interest and offered a minimal deal for him to stay. The Kansas City Chiefs kicked the tires, as did the Detroit Lions, Brees recalled.

All of a sudden, Brees needed the Saints as much as they needed him.

Not even the Saints could have imagined how well things would turn out, with Brees coming back stronger and better than ever, leading the Saints to the NFC championship game in his first season and Super Bowl XLIV during the 2009 season. During his four years in New Orleans, he already had thrown for more than 15,000 yards and 100 touchdown passes.

Brees, his wife and their 9-month-old son, Baylen, decided to live in Uptown, where they restored a 100-year-old house. That felt like the real New Orleans to them, and they wanted to embrace their new community with open arms.

Brees talked once again at the Lusher dedication about how quickly and eagerly the city embraced him and Brittany, and how much they said the feeling was mutual.

He went from knowing very little about the city to feeling as though he was "100 percent" a part of the community.

"I'm proud to call myself a New Orleanian," Brees said.

DREW CHRISTOPHER BREES BORN **January 15, 1979**, in Austin, Texas HEIGHT **6 feet** WEIGHT **209 lbs.**

15 GAMES	**15** STARTED	**363** COMPLETIONS	**514** ATTEMPTS	**70.6** PERCENTAGE	**4,388** YARDS

MICHAEL DeMOCKER/THE TIMES-PICAYUNE

ATTENDED **Westlake High School, Purdue University**   NFL EXPERIENCE **Nine seasons**

| **8.5** | **34** | **11** | **20** | **135** | **109.6** |
| AVERAGE | TOUCHDOWNS | INTERCEPTIONS | SACKS | YARDS LOST (SACKS) | RATING |

SAINTS | BILLS

27 | 7

Defensive lineman Anthony Hargrove and the rest of the Saints pushed their weight around against the Bills.

MICHAEL DeMOCKER / THE TIMES-PICAYUNE

SUPER SAINTS

23

GAME 3 SEPTEMBER 27, 2009 BUFFALO

SAINTS | BILLS

27   **7**

OFF & RUNNING

The Saints keep the Bills in check, and running back Pierre Thomas lifts N.O.

By Mike Triplett Staff writer

Superman quarterback Drew Brees was grounded by an aggressive Buffalo Bills defense and a fickle wind.

But the Saints soared anyway in a 27-7 victory over Buffalo in Orchard Park, N.Y., getting a lift from their defense, special teams and rejuvenated running back Pierre Thomas.

In many respects, it was the team's most impressive victory since the 2006 season, with Brees being held to 172 yards passing — his lowest total since 2006 — and, for the first time in the past 12 games, no touchdowns.

"This is a game in the past that, unfortunately, probably would not have gone our way, you know?" Brees said of a slugfest that was stuck at 10-7 with 10 minutes remaining.

"You can call it the lucky breaks, but I think even more so than that, it's the attitude," Brees said, smiling when he was reminded that the team's slogan this year was "Finish."

"Absolutely," he said.

Now the Saints needed to apply that motto to the rest of this season, as they hoped to turn their first 3-0 start since '06 into their first playoff appearance since that season.

Up next in seven days was a showdown at the Superdome against another 3-0 team, the upstart New York Jets, who were guided by aggressive defensive-minded coach Rex Ryan.

Based on their performance against Buffalo, New Orleans was ready for the challenge.

"It's important for us as a team to have wins like this," Saints right tackle Jon Stinchcomb said of a rare victory that came on the road in brisk weather conditions against a physical opponent that brought consistent pressure.

The Saints rushed for 222 yards against the Bills — including a career-high 126 from Thomas, all of which came in the second half.

New Orleans held Buffalo to 89 yards rushing and 243 yards of total offense, while racking up four sacks and forcing one interception and nine punts. The Bills were

Pierre Thomas finds the hole and leaves the Bills in his wake. He rushed for 126 yards in the second half.

BILLS	1ST 0	2ND 7	3RD 0	4TH 0	F 7
SAINTS	7	3	0	17	27

3-0

RECORD AFTER GAME 3

GAME STATISTICS
Attendance: 70,261 at Ralph Wilson Stadium

SCORING SUMMARY

1ST **SAINTS:** Lynell Hamilton 1-yard run (John Carney kick). Ten plays, 82 yards in 4:56.

2ND **BILLS:** Ryan Denney 25-yard pass from Brian Moorman (Rian Lindell kick). Nine plays, 72 yards in 3:26.
SAINTS: Carney 27-yard field goal. Five plays, 23 yards in 1:55.

3RD **NO SCORING**

4TH **SAINTS:** Pierre Thomas 34-yard run (Carney kick). Three plays, 66 yards in 1:16.
SAINTS: Carney 35-yard field goal. Nine plays, 49 yards in 4:01.
SAINTS: Pierre Thomas 19-yard run (Carney kick). Two plays, 25 yards in 12 seconds.

INDIVIDUAL STATISTICS

RUSHING
SAINTS: Pierre Thomas 14-126, Reggie Bush 13-64.
BILLS: Fred Jackson 18-71, Trent Edwards 2-13.

PASSING
SAINTS: Drew Brees 16-26-172-0-0.
BILLS: Trent Edwards 20-35-156-0-1; Brian Moorman 1-1-25-1-0.

RECEIVING
SAINTS: Jeremy Shockey 6-48, Marques Colston 4-67.
BILLS: Josh Reed 6-60, Derek Fine 5-34.

INTERCEPTIONS
SAINTS: Will Smith 1.
BILLS: none.

SACKS
SAINTS: Charles Grant 1.5, Sedrick Ellis 1, Will Smith 1, Randall Gay 0.5.
BILLS: Chris Kelsay 1, Aaron Schobel 1.

TACKLES (unassisted)
SAINTS: Jabari Greer 6, Roman Harper 6.
BILLS: Chris Kelsay 6, Bryan Scott 5.

TEAM STATISTICS

	SAINTS	BILLS
FIRST DOWNS	21	13
TOTAL OFFENSIVE PLAYS-YARDS (NET)	69-378	61-243
RUSHES-YARDS (NET)	38-222	21-89
PASSING YARDS (NET)	156	154
PASSES (COMP-ATT-INT)	16-29-0	21-36-1
PUNTS (NUMBER-AVG)	5-42.6	9-46.6
PUNT RETURNS-YARDS	4-17	3-1
KICKOFF RETURNS-YARDS	2-16	5-111
PENALTY YARDS	9-97	12-116
FUMBLES-LOST	1-1	1-1
TIME OF POSSESSION	33:34	26:26
FIELD GOALS (ATT-MADE)	2-2	0-0

Saints defensive end Will Smith, with some help from corner-back Randall Gay, intercepts a pass thrown by Trent Edwards.

MICHAEL DeMOCKER / THE TIMES-PICAYUNE

DAVID GRUNFELD / THE TIMES-PICAYUNE
Linebacker Scott Fujita (55) and defensive tackle Sedrick Ellis make life miserable for Buffalo quarterback Trent Edwards.

2-for-14 on third-down conversions.

Rookie Malcolm Jenkins forced a fumble on special teams, and the Saints won the turnover battle (2-1) for the third consecutive game.

New Orleans Coach Sean Payton awarded a game ball to defensive coordinator Gregg Williams, who served as head coach of the Bills from 2001 to 2003.

Williams made his triumphant return, pestering the Bills' no-huddle offense with a 3-4 front and more zone blitzes than he had shown in the first two games combined.

The Bills' touchdown came on a fake field goal in the first quarter, when holder/punter Brian Moorman threw a 25-yard scoring pass to wide-open defensive end Ryan Denney.

The Saints were especially impressive up front, with ends Will Smith and Charles Grant and tackle Sedrick Ellis each earning at least a sack. The Saints were credited with 14 quarterback hits, and Buffalo's top receiving target, Terrell Owens, didn't catch a pass. Fellow big-play threat Lee Evans caught four passes for 31 yards.

"Coach Payton challenged our defensive line saying this is a game we had an advantage in," Smith said, referring to the Bills' inexperienced offensive line.

Smith, in particular, answered that challenge with one of his most active games in seasons. He stuffed tailback Fred Jackson for a 3-yard loss on third-and-1 to force a punt in the first quarter, and he sacked Trent Edwards on third-and-4 to force a punt early in the fourth quarter.

But his most impressive play was in the third quarter, when he leaped to intercept a ball that was tipped by cornerback Jabari Greer, ending the Bills' drive deep in Saints' territory.

It was Smith's first career interception, and he said it probably was the highest he has jumped since he performed the vertical leap test at the NFL Scouting Combine coming out of Ohio State.

What was most impressive about the defense's performance was that it was so necessary, with the Saints clinging to a three-point lead for most of the afternoon.

Carney added a field goal and Thomas a touchdown run in the game's final four minutes.

"Once we got in the third quarter, still 10-7, offensively we were thinking, 'We've got to close this thing out. Our defense is playing their butt off, and we've got to do something,'" Brees said. "And, obviously, that's when the Pierre show began."

SUPER SAINTS

27

SAINTS
24

JETS
10

New Orleans receiver Robert
Meachem clears a path for
running back Reggie Bush
against the Jets.

DAVID GRUNFELD / THE TIMES-PICAYUNE

SAINTS | JETS
24 · 10

SHARPER IMAGE

Safety Darren Sharper's two interceptions highlight New Orleans' winning effort against dazed and confused New York

By Brian Allee–Walsh Staff writer

For the better part of a week, a lot of pregame hype centered around the New York Jets and their loquacious blitz-minded coach, Rex Ryan.

Before a raucous sellout crowd of 70,009 at the Superdome, the "no-name" Saints' defense coached by veteran coordinator Gregg Williams got the last word, providing the impetus in a crucial 24-10 victory to remain unbeaten and atop the NFC South.

Williams' swarming, gritty, hands-on group of defenders helped stake the Black & Gold to a 17-0 lead with two touchdowns in the first six minutes of the second quarter, and the Saints now found themselves 4-0 for the third time in franchise history.

New Orleans free safety Darren Sharper continued his thieving ways, returning one of his two interceptions 99 yards for a touchdown, and defensive tackle Remi Ayodele recovered a fumble in the end zone for his first NFL score.

In all, the Saints collected four turnovers to push their league-leading total to 13.

"I can quote Gregg Williams. It's not about the Xs and Os," New Orleans cornerback Jabari Greer said of the first-year defensive coordinator. "It's about players making plays, and that's what we did. That's what he gives us, the equipment to go out there and make plays. If we made a statement today, that was it."

Said Ryan, whose team had yielded 33 points in its 3-0 start: "The Saints outplayed us today. Overall, it was a poor performance on our part. We kind of got it handed to us a little bit."

New Orleans needed every point provided by the defense, as quarterback Drew Brees and the offense struggled for the second consecutive game, producing 10 points and squandering several opportunities.

After throwing nine touchdown passes in the first seven quarters this season, Brees had thrown none in the past nine.

Saints safety Darren Sharper rejoices after picking off his second interception of Jets quarterback Mark Sanchez.

KATHY ANDERSON / THE TIMES-PICAYUNE

	1ST	2ND	3RD	4TH	F
JETS	0	3	7	0	10
SAINTS	3	14	0	7	24

4-0

RECORD AFTER GAME 4

SCORING SUMMARY

1ST **SAINTS:** John Carney 34-yard field goal. Thirteen plays, 60 yards in 6:54.

2ND **SAINTS:** Darren Sharper 99-yard interception return (Carney kick).
SAINTS: Remi Ayodele fumble recovery in end zone (Carney kick).
JETS: Jay Feely 38-yard field goal. Fourteen plays, 60 yards in 7:12.

3RD **JETS:** Thomas Jones 15-yard run (Feely kick). Four plays, 34 yards in 1:16.

4TH **SAINTS:** Pierre Thomas 1-yard run (Carney kick). Eleven plays, 74 yards in 6:49.

TEAM STATISTICS

	SAINTS	JETS
FIRST DOWNS	18	14
TOTAL OFFENSIVE PLAYS-YARDS (NET)	64-343	58-244
RUSHES-YARDS (NET)	32-153	27-132
PASSING YARDS (NET)	190	112
PASSES (COMP-ATT-INT)	20-32-0	14-27-3
PUNTS (NUMBER-AVG)	5-38.0	6-42.0
PUNT RETURNS-YARDS	1-22	0-0
KICKOFF RETURNS-YARDS	1-26	1-17
PENALTY YARDS	7-70	3-21
FUMBLES-LOST	2-1	1-1
TIME OF POSSESSION	32:39	27:21
FIELD GOALS (ATT-MADE)	1-1	1-1

INDIVIDUAL STATISTICS

RUSHING
SAINTS: Pierre Thomas 19-86, Reggie Bush 6-37.
JETS: Thomas Jones 13-48, Mark Sanchez 4-24.

MATTHEW HINTON / THE TIMES-PICAYUNE
Running back Pierre Thomas breaks through the Jets' defense.

PASSING
SAINTS: Drew Brees 20-32-190-0-0.
JETS: Mark Sanchez 14-27-138-0-3.

RECEIVING
SAINTS: Pierre Thomas 4-46, Jeremy Shockey 4-34.
JETS: Jerricho Cotchery 5-71, Leon Washington 4-24.

INTERCEPTIONS
SAINTS: Darren Sharper 2, Randall Gay 1.
JETS: none.

SACKS
SAINTS: Charles Grant 2, Will Smith 2.
JETS: none.

TACKLES (unassisted)
SAINTS: Jabari Greer 6, Roman Harper 6.
JETS: David Harris 10, Kerry Rhodes 8.

SUPER SAINTS

MICHAEL DeMOCKER / THE TIMES-PICAYUNE

Saints defensive tackle Remi Ayodele (92) races to recover a fumble in the end zone in the second quarter for his first NFL score.

"After we drove down the field on our first possession of the game — we got three points, we very well could have seven — it was about managing the football game," said Brees, who completed 20 of 32 passes for 190 yards, with no interceptions, no sacks and a 78.9 passer rating.

Said Saints Coach Sean Payton: "This isn't about style points. This is about the formula to win each game and then get on to the next week."

Brees' counterpart, Jets rookie quarterback Mark Sanchez, gave the Saints a huge helping hand with four turnovers — two resulting in touchdowns for New Orleans.

Sanchez's first mistake ended up in Sharper's hands at the Saints' 1-yard line on the first play of the second quarter, and 99 yards later New Orleans led 10-0.

"I don't want to say that he eyed his receivers," said Sharper, who now had 59 career interceptions and led the NFL with five. "I would say that one of my strengths is reading quarterbacks and knowing where they are trying to throw the football."

Sanchez attempted to squeeze the ball into tight end Dustin Keller, but Sharper played the role of center fielder beautifully and made an easy interception in stride.

"That's a classic mistake by a rookie quarterback looking at his receiver," said Sanchez, who completed 14 of 27 passes for 138 yards, with no touchdowns and three interceptions — for a 27.0 passer rating. "Sharper read me the

entire way. He saw my eyes, and I threw it right to him."

Sanchez added to his woes by getting called for a personal foul while trying to make a tackle on Sharper in front of the Jets' bench.

"It was a cheap shot," said Saints middle linebacker Jonathan Vilma, the victim of Sanchez's low blow to the knees. "I don't know why he did it to be honest with you."

Sanchez's second turnover came minutes later after the Saints failed to score from a first-and-goal at New York's 1.

With the Jets facing second-and-7 from their 2, New Orleans right defensive end Will Smith beat left tackle D'Brickashaw Ferguson and stripped the ball from Sanchez's grasp. Ayodele beat Vilma to the loose ball in the end zone, extending the Saints' lead to 17-0 with nine minutes remaining in the first half.

"That was huge," said Ayodele, who had started the past three games for injured starter Kendrick Clancy. "We noticed that (Sanchez) runs around with the ball real loosely in his hands. When I saw it on tape, it was like he must have some big hands the way he runs around with it out there. So we knew if we could get to him we could probably get that ball out."

Then, with a big grin, Ayodele gave the rest of the story.

"Vilma tried to steal it from me, actually," Ayodele said. "I didn't know it was him. I thought it was one of the other players. I just snatched it back."

The Giants are only casual
observers as New Orleans
receiver Marques Colston hauls
in a 12-yard touchdown pass.
MICHAEL DeMOCKER / THE TIMES-PICAYUNE

SAINTS | GIANTS
48 **27**

GAME 5 OCTOBER 18, 2009 SUPERDOME

SAINTS | GIANTS
48 | 27

HIGH FIVE

The Saints' unstoppable offense and their opportunistic defense once again take another Giant leap forward

By Mike Triplett Staff writer

The Saints hopped on a plane to Miami later in the week following their game against the New York Giants for a regular-season date with the Dolphins.

The way they were playing, they also looked to head back to Miami for Super Bowl XLIV on Feb. 7.

New Orleans gave their most impressive performance of the season against the Giants — quite possibly one of the best in franchise history — as the Saints overwhelmed previously unbeaten New York 48-27 at the Superdome.

"Our ability to remain focused coming off the bye week, playing one of the best teams in the NFC, and to win the way that we did, that says a lot about the guys that we have, the coaching staff that we have and our mentality," said New Orleans quarterback Drew Brees, who revived his MVP campaign with a vintage performance (he completed 23 of 30 passes for 369 yards, with four touchdown passes and no interceptions).

He spread the love around, though, in a game when the Saints' defense and running game also stood toe to toe with the big, bad Giants (5-1) and knocked them out.

"What can I say? Everybody showed up," said Brees as New Orleans moved to 5-0. "The fans were awesome. The defense played great. Our offense, we did what we had to do — and it ended up being a big victory."

Seven players scored touchdowns for the Saints, something that was accomplished 10 times by any NFL team since the 1970 merger. And they won the turnover battle (2-0), making it a forgettable homecoming game for Giants quarterback Eli Manning, who was a standout at Newman School.

As exuberant as the Saints were in the postgame locker room, though, they were careful not to overplay the significance of any win in mid-October.

Fullback Heath Evans said he believed in the idea of "statement games" — just not this early in the season.

"We haven't accomplished any of our goals yet," said

Safety Roman Harper sacks the Giants' Eli Manning, who attended Newman School, and scrambles to the ball.
MICHAEL DeMOCKER / THE TIMES-PICAYUNE

GIANTS	1ST 3	2ND 14	3RD 0	4TH 10	F 27
SAINTS	14	20	7	7	48

5-0

RECORD AFTER GAME 5

INDIVIDUAL STATISTICS

RUSHING

SAINTS: Pierre Thomas 15-72, Mike Bell 15-34.
GIANTS: Ahmad Bradshaw 10-48, Brandon Jacobs 7-33.

The Saints' defense comes up with another giant play against New York as New Orleans improves to 5-0.

PASSING

SAINTS: Drew Brees 23-30-369-4-0.
GIANTS: Eli Manning 14-31-178-1-1, David Carr 4-5-72-1-0.

RECEIVING

SAINTS: Marques Colston 8-166, Lance Moore 6-78.
GIANTS: Hakeem Nicks 5-114, Mario Manningham 4-50.

INTERCEPTIONS

SAINTS: Jabari Greer 1.
GIANTS: none.

SACKS

SAINTS: Remi Ayodele 1, Roman Harper 1.
GIANTS: none.

TACKLES (unassisted)

SAINTS: Jabari Greer 5, Roman Harper 4.
GIANTS: C.C. Brown 12, Chase Blackburn 8.

GAME STATISTICS
Attendance: 69,719 at Superdome

SCORING SUMMARY

1ST
SAINTS: Mike Bell 2-yard run (John Carney kick). Fifteen plays, 70 yards in 7:41.
SAINTS: Jeremy Shockey 1-yard pass from Drew Brees (Carney kick). Six plays, 80 yards in 2:48.
GIANTS: Lawrence Tynes 49-yard field goal. Six plays, 19 yards in 2:08.

2ND
SAINTS: Robert Meachem 36-yard pass from Brees (extra-point attempt blocked). Four plays, 57 yards in 2:23.
GIANTS: Ahmad Bradshaw 10-yard run (Tynes kick). Nine plays, 73 yards in 4:59.
SAINTS: Lance Moore 12-yard pass from Brees (Carney kick). Five plays, 61 yards 2:37.
GIANTS: Mario Manningham 15-yard pass from Eli Manning (Tynes kick). Four plays, 37 yards in 1:45.
SAINTS: Reggie Bush 7-yard run (Carney kick). Two plays, 7 yards in nine seconds.

3RD
SAINTS: Marques Colston 12-yard pass from Brees (Carney kick). Nine plays, 71 yards at 5:11.

4TH
GIANTS: Tynes 38-yard field goal. Eleven plays, 60 yards in 2:43.
SAINTS: Heath Evans 2-yard run (Carney kick). Eight plays, 80 yards in 5:05.
GIANTS: Hakeem Nicks 37-yard pass from David Carr (Tynes kick). Three plays, 50 yards in one minute.

TEAM STATISTICS

	SAINTS	GIANTS
FIRST DOWNS	28	17
TOTAL OFFENSIVE PLAYS-YARDS (NET)	70-493	57-325
RUSHES-YARDS (NET)	40-124	19-84
PASSING YARDS (NET)	369	241
PASSES (COMP-ATT-INT)	23-30-0	18-36-1
PUNTS (NUMBER-AVG)	4-45.0	4-46.5
PUNT RETURNS-YARDS	2-0	2-51
KICKOFF RETURNS-YARDS	4-91	8-230
PENALTY YARDS	6-55	9-110
FUMBLES-LOST	1-0	1-1
TIME OF POSSESSION	36:07	23:53
FIELD GOALS (ATT-MADE)	0-0	2-2

SUSAN POAG / THE TIMES-PICAYUNE

Saints fullback Heath Evans lets out a roar after scoring on a 2-yard run in the fourth quarter against New York, with tight end Jeremy Shockey, right, joining in on the fun.

Evans, who pointed out that New Orleans hadn't played its first NFC South opponent, and winning the division was the first item on its list.

"This week, we'll talk about the win — and there will be more talked about it," Saints Coach Sean Payton said. "But in about four or five weeks, it will just be a win."

Linebacker Jonathan Vilma said that attitude was evidence of how much faith New Orleans had in itself, even before this latest command performance.

"The confidence was always there," Vilma said. "And you notice, or if you didn't you should notice, we don't get too excited about the wins. We're happy about it, then we come back to work on Wednesday."

No one exemplified that attitude more than Brees, who was furious on the sideline after he threw an incomplete pass on third-and-2 early in the third quarter — even though the Saints were leading 34-17, and it was their first punt.

Right tackle Jon Stinchcomb laughed about how upset Brees was later in the game after he completed a 34-yard pass to Robert Meachem that wound up at the 2-yard line instead of the end zone.

"I said, 'Drew, we're at the 2.' But he was upset about some route or something," Stinchcomb said. "And that's just the type of guy he is. He's always working to be the best that he can, and it's not about his glory but to make

sure this team is in the best situation he can put us in."

As usual, Brees put the Saints in a great situation during the opening drive, marching New Orleans 70 yards on 15 plays before running back Mike Bell leaped over the pile for a 2-yard touchdown run on fourth-and-1.

The Saints had scored points on their opening drive in every game this season, and they had never trailed.

"As I recall on that first drive, we converted a couple critical third downs to keep the drive going, then ended up going for it on fourth down to get the touchdown," Brees said.

The momentum never turned.

New Orleans scored touchdowns on its first four possessions — including a 1-yard pass to Jeremy Shockey, a 36-yard pass to Meachem and a 12-yard pass to Lance Moore — to take a 27-10 lead.

"Obviously, we could not stop them," New York Coach Tom Coughlin said. "We could not get them out."

Said safety Darren Sharper: "This definitely was a game that you can say will open up some eyes for people that questioned how good the Saints are. It is a big statement for us. You can enjoy it and bask in it a little bit, beating a team that's 5-0, that was the No. 1 seed in the NFC last year and the Super Bowl champions two years ago. So it lets you know you were good, but we knew we were good."

SUPER SAINTS

39

SAINTS | DOLPHINS
46 34

Tracy Porter's 54-yard interception return in the fourth quarter
punctuates New Orleans' furious comeback against Miami.

G. ANDREW BOYD / THE TIMES-PICAYUNE

SUPER SAINTS

41

SAINTS | DOLPHINS

46   **34**

GUTS & GLORY

With New Orleans floundering, quarterback Drew Brees emphatically takes over in a miraculous win against Miami

By Brian Allee–Walsh Staff writer

As the sun began to set on the Saints' perfect season late in the first half against the Miami Dolphins at Land Shark Stadium, quarterback Drew Brees made an impassioned plea on the sideline to Coach Sean Payton.

Trailing 24-3 with five seconds remaining in the first half and the ball resting inside Miami's 1-yard line, New Orleans' John Carney stood on the right hash mark, staring down a potential 19-yard field-goal attempt.

Unbeknownst to Carney and the field-goal unit, Payton had a pit bull gnawing on his ear.

"I just told Coach, 'I'll get it. We got 6 inches, I'll get it,' " Brees said.

To which Payton replied: "You better."

Brees made good on his promise, scoring on a 1-yard sneak to jump-start one of the most dramatic comebacks in franchise history.

From that point forward, the Saints kept chopping wood until by game's end they had brought the breathless Dolphins to their knees, winning 46-34 in Miami and keeping alive their dreams of an unbeaten season and perhaps a return trip to this stadium and Super Bowl XLIV on Feb. 7.

"Wouldn't that be wonderful," Saints owner Tom Benson said in a jubilant locker room. "We've still got a long way to go, but we're working on it. For us to be down like that at halftime and come back is unbelievable. That says our team is really a team."

Cornerback Tracy Porter sealed the deal with 1:53 remaining on a 54-yard interception return for a touchdown, increasing the Saints' lead to the final 12-point margin and enabling General Manager Mickey Loomis to breathe a sigh of relief.

It was New Orleans' sixth consecutive double-digit win in as many games this season and made them the team to beat in the NFC.

"That was a strong win, a strong, strong, strong win," Loomis said. "What made it a good win is that we had four or five chances to cash it in, and they didn't. That

When the Saints needed it most, quarterback
Drew Brees delivers, scoring on a 1-yard
sneak just before halftime.
ELIOT KAMENITZ / THE TIMES-PICAYUNE

DOLPHINS	1ST 14	2ND 10	3RD 10	4TH 0	F 34
SAINTS	3	7	14	22	46

6-0

RECORD AFTER GAME 6

INDIVIDUAL STATISTICS

RUSHING

SAINTS: Mike Bell 12-80, Pierre Thomas 8-30.
DOLPHINS: Ricky Williams 9-80, Ronnie Brown 16-48.

Wanting to help out, Saints tight end David Thomas pushes running back Reggie Bush forward for extra yards.

ELIOT KAMENITZ / THE TIMES-PICAYUNE

PASSING

SAINTS: Drew Brees 22-38-298-1-3.
DOLPHINS: Chad Henne 18-36-211-0-2, Ronnie Brown 0-1-0-0-0.

RECEIVING

SAINTS: Marques Colston 5-72, Jeremy Shockey 4-105.
DOLPHINS: Greg Camarillo 5-55, Brian Hartline 3-94.

INTERCEPTIONS

SAINTS: Tracy Porter 1, Darren Sharper 1.
DOLPHINS: Tyrone Culver 1, Nathan Jones 1, Reggie Torbor 1.

SACKS

SAINTS: Anthony Hargrove 2.
DOLPHINS: Yeremiah Bell 1.5, Phillip Merling 0.5, Joey Porter 0.5, Randy Starks 0.5, Jason Taylor 2.

TACKLES (unassisted)

SAINTS: Jonathan Vilma 7, Tracy Porter 6.
DOLPHINS: Yeremiah Bell 8, Gibril Wilson 7.

GAME STATISTICS

Attendance: 66,689 at Land Shark Stadium

SCORING SUMMARY

1ST
DOLPHINS: Ricky Williams 4-yard run (Dan Carpenter kick). One play, 4 yards in five seconds.
SAINTS: John Carney 46-yard field goal. Four plays, 7 yards in 2:14.
DOLPHINS: Williams 68-yard run (Carpenter kick). One play, 63 yards in 19 seconds.

2ND
DOLPHINS: Carpenter 32-yard field goal. Twelve plays, 46 yards in 7:24.
DOLPHINS: Ronnie Brown 8-yard run (Carpenter kick). Four plays, 19 yards in 2:05.
SAINTS: Drew Brees 1-yard run (Carney kick). Eight plays, 51 yards in 1:36.

3RD
SAINTS: Darren Sharper 42-yard interception return (Carney kick).
DOLPHINS: Carpenter 33-yard field goal. Four plays, 0 yards in 1:18.
SAINTS: Marques Colston 10-yard pass (Carney kick). Eight plays, 82 yards in 4:50.
DOLPHINS: Williams 4-yard run (Carpenter kick). Three plays, 79 yards in 1:40.

4TH
SAINTS: Reggie Bush 10-yard run (Carney kick). Three plays, 79 yards in 1:40.
SAINTS: Brees 2-yard run (extra-point attempt failed). Eight plays, 60 yards in 4:17.
SAINTS: Carney 20-yard field goal. Ten plays, 64 yards in 4:38.
SAINTS: Tracy Porter 54-yard interception return (two-point conversion attempt failed).

TEAM STATISTICS

	SAINTS	DOLPHINS
FIRST DOWNS	22	17
TOTAL OFFENSIVE PLAYS-YARDS (NET)	70-414	69-334
RUSHES-YARDS (NET)	27-138	30-137
PASSING YARDS (NET)	276	197
PASSES (COMP-ATT-INT)	22-38-3	18-37-2
PUNTS (NUMBER-AVG)	3-45.7	6-46.7
PUNT RETURNS-YARDS	5-23	3-26
KICKOFF RETURNS-YARDS	6-185	5-112
PENALTY YARDS	6-25	8-55
FUMBLES-LOST	2-1	1-1
TIME OF POSSESSION	33:02	26:58
FIELD GOALS (ATT-MADE)	3-2	2-2

ELIOT KAMENITZ / THE TIMES-PICAYUNE
New Orleans' Reggie Bush scores on a 10-yard run that displayed his talents for finding the end zone.

was a good character win."

The victory matched the Saints' biggest comeback in franchise history, tying their 21-point turnarounds in a 41-24 victory against the Cincinnati Bengals on Dec. 20, 1987, and their 43-38 win against the San Francisco 49ers on Nov. 23, 1969, according to the Elias Sports Bureau.

It also allowed New Orleans to improve to 6-0 for the second-best start in franchise history, trailing only the 1991 team that opened 7-0.

With the Minnesota Vikings' 27-17 loss to the Pittsburgh Steelers, the Saints were the lone undefeated team in the NFC and one of three in the NFL (Indianapolis Colts and Denver Broncos also were 6-0). It was the first time in NFL history that three teams were unbeaten after seven weeks.

The Black & Gold stayed unbeaten after easily playing their worst half of football this season and the Dolphins perhaps their best. The usually accurate and sure-handed Brees accounted for three turnovers in the first half, resulting in 14 points for Miami.

Until this game, the Saints had never trailed this season.

"Hey, they have No. 9 (Brees) back there," Dolphins cornerback Vontae Davis said. "That is a guy who can take over a game."

For the first 23 minutes, Miami ran its Wildcat offense to perfection, alternating its battering rams/run-

ning backs Ricky Williams and Ronnie Brown down the throat of a Saints defense that seemed outwitted from the outset.

Williams, a former Saint, scored on runs of 4 and 68 yards, Brown ran 8 yards for another touchdown, and Dan Carpenter made a 32-yard field goal for a 24-3 lead with 8:55 remaining in the first half.

Based on the final 39 minutes, New Orleans apparently had the Dolphins right where it wanted them.

"Despite being down 24-3, we still felt good about our chances because everything had gone wrong for us, and we were still in the game," said Brees, who rebounded from a slow start to complete 22 of 38 passes for 298 yards, with one touchdown and three interceptions for a meager passer rating of 58.9.

Saints free safety Darren Sharper continued his impressive play, returning a Chad Henne interception 42 yards for a touchdown in the first 64 seconds of the third quarter. Sharper increased his interceptions to six and his pick-six total to three — both league highs.

"This is a huge win," New Orleans linebacker Scott Shanle said. "It can be a season-changing win. When you look back over the course of a season, a win like this can be huge — and it says a lot about the character of the team.

"This was a test we hadn't faced yet, and we came back and responded."

With the Saints needing a big lift, quarterback Drew Brees delivers and soars after rushing for a touchdown.

SAINTS | DOLPHINS
46   34

Saints summon the will and find their way in a performance that defies belief

JEFF DUNCAN

Mostly in private and occasionally in public, the Saints had tossed around the word "special" to describe their remarkable start to the 2009 season.

Even before the first kickoff of the season, quarterback Drew Brees commissioned T-shirts with the word in big block letters across the back — SPECIAL — and distributed them around the locker room to teammates.

Now we knew why.

If any doubts remained that the Saints were in the midst of one of the truly special seasons in club history, they melted in the sultry South Florida heat and white-hot fury of their stunning come-from-behind victory against the Miami Dolphins.

Even the most cynical Who Dats must have converted to devout believers after watching the Saints outscore the shocked Dolphins 43-10 in the head-spinning final 30:02 of their 46-34 victory at Land Shark Stadium.

It was New Orleans' sixth consecutive win by double digits and left the Saints as the lone unbeaten team in the NFC. They were 6-0 for only the second time in franchise history, and you had to go back almost two decades to find a better start to a Saints season. The 1991 bunch won their first seven.

"We have a great locker room, a great team — and we stuck by each other," running back Mike Bell said. "We had a great attitude coming into halftime. We weren't feeling sorry for ourselves."

Everyone, including myself, thought this was a classic "trap" game for the Saints. Sandwiched between an emotional victory against the unbeaten New York Giants last week and an upcoming "Monday Night Football" showdown against the rival Atlanta Falcons, it seemed the perfect recipe for a letdown. The game was on the road, and it was in the South Florida heat — in a place where New Orleans had never won a game.

And indeed, the Saints opened against Miami as if they had spent the night before partying on South Beach.

They — not the Dolphins — looked like fish out of water as they stumbled and bumbled through the first 28 minutes.

New Orleans committed three penalties before it made its fifth offensive snap, and the Saints couldn't stop the run on defense and couldn't protect quarterback

Drew Brees on offense.

Late in the second quarter, the Saints weren't in a trap, they were in a chasm. The Dolphins led 24-3, and they were driving for another score just before halftime.

Then, seemingly from nowhere, there was a spark.

On a seemingly benign pass in the right flat, safety Roman Harper made a diving stop and stripped the football from receiver Davone Bess, and Scott Shanle fell on it. The Saints had their first break, and they had life.

A few plays later, Brees looked like the Dolphins logo as he leapt over pile into the end zone for the Saints' first touchdown. It was a do or die play from the one-foot line with five seconds remaining in the half and no timeouts.

New Orleans' defense came through again on the first series of the second half. Safety Darren Sharper's third interception return for a touchdown made the score 24-17, and from that point it was all Saints.

"I was just proud of the way we hung in there and hung in there," Payton said. "We talked about playing a full game — four quarters — and I think we did that today."

Their 238 points was the second highest total in NFL history for a team in the first six games. Only the 2000 St. Louis Rams, who scored 262, had posted more.

The Saints scored 45 or more points in a game five times in the first 642 games of club history. They now had done it four times this season, and none in more incredible fashion than against Miami.

New Orleans entered the game having not trailed in any of their first five games. Yet against the Dolphins, the Saints found themselves behind for most of the game. They trailed from the seven-minute mark of the first quarter until 8:35 of the fourth quarter.

That was when Brees snuck into the end zone from the 2-yard line to put the Saints on top for good and continue their quixotic quest during this seeming season of destiny.

After Brees scored, he bolted to his feet, coiled his 6-foot frame toward the turf and vaulted skyward to dunk the ball over the goal post.

"That's all we've talked about, finishing football games," Brees said. "We hadn't been in a situation like this in a while. . . . We all knew that they had given us their best shot . . . and all we had to do is string a few drives together. . . we knew it was going to happen, and sure enough it did."

SAINTS | FALCONS

35 27

SUPER SAINTS

Defensive end Will
Smith (top) and
lineman Anthony
Hargrove sack —
make that flatten
— the Falcons'
Matt Ryan.

MICHAEL DEMOCKER /
THE TIMES-PICAYUNE

New Orleans running back Pierre Thomas
isn't denied and scores on an acrobatic
1-yard touchdown reception.
MICHAEL DeMOCKER / THE TIMES-PICAYUNE

SAINTS | FALCONS
35   **27**

STILL SOARING

The Saints top the Falcons on 'Monday Night Football' to equal their best start in franchise history at 7-0

By Mike Triplett Staff writer

The Saints weren't perfect on "Monday Night Football," as they outlasted the division-rival Atlanta Falcons for a sometimes sloppy, sometimes spectacular 35-27 victory at the Superdome.

But their performance was perfectly acceptable as they matched the best start in franchise history at 7-0.

"This is a huge win," quarterback Drew Brees said. "We knew this coming in, obviously, you win and really it's worth two (in the NFC South standings). It wasn't the prettiest win at times, but we did what we needed to do when we needed to do it. That says a lot."

New Orleans now had opened a three-game lead in the division, with Atlanta (4-3) the closest contender. Although it was too early to make postseason promises, a graphic flashed on the screen during ESPN's telecast that pointed out that the Saints had the easiest remaining schedule in the NFL in the next nine weeks.

"We haven't hit the halfway point of the season yet," Saints Coach Sean Payton said when the undefeated talk was mentioned. "Each week we get another challenge, so we're just focused on trying to get better. And each time we play another game, it seems to have that much more importance."

Up next for the Saints in six days was another division matchup against the Carolina Panthers (3-4), who were coming off an impressive victory over the Arizona Cardinals.

But with all due respect to Payton, New Orleans' win against the Falcons was bigger than a typical matchup.

Atlanta, which beat out the Saints for a playoff spot last season, loomed as New Orleans' strongest contender in the NFC South this season, and a Falcons victory would have closed the gap to one game in the division race.

The Falcons didn't relent. They forced four turnovers and piled up 442 yards of offense — outgaining the Saints by 5 yards.

Once again, however, New Orleans' big-play defense

FALCONS 1ST **14** 2ND **0** 3RD **7** 4TH **6** F **27**
SAINTS **7** **21** **0** **7** **35**

7-0

RECORD AFTER GAME 7

INDIVIDUAL STATISTICS

RUSHING
SAINTS: Pierre Thomas 14-91, Mike Bell 17-49.
FALCONS: Michael Turner 20-151, Matt Ryan 3-9.

PASSING
SAINTS: Drew Brees 25-33-308-2-1.
FALCONS: Matt Ryan 19-42-289-1-3.

RECEIVING
SAINTS: Marques Colston 6-85, Jeremy Shockey 5-72.
FALCONS: Tony Gonzalez 6-89, Roddy White 4-108.

MICHAEL DeMOCKER/ THE TIMES-PICAYUNE
Following Saints cornerback Jabari Greer's interception, defensive lineman Anthony Hargrove gives him a hand.

INTERCEPTIONS
SAINTS: Jabari Greer 1, Tracy Porter 1, Darren Porter 1.
FALCONS: Brent Grimes 1.

SACKS
SAINTS: Will Smith 2, Anthony Hargrove 1.
FALCONS: Jonathan Babineaux 1, Thomas DeCoud 1.

TACKLES (unassisted)
SAINTS: Roman Harper 7, Tracy Porter 6.
FALCONS: Curtis Lofton 12, Erik Coleman 6.

GAME STATISTICS
Attendance: 70,088 at Superdome

SCORING SUMMARY

1ST
FALCONS: Michael Turner 13-yard run (Jason Elam kick). Eight plays, 77 yards in 3:57.
SAINTS: Pierre Thomas 22-yard run (John Carney kick). Ten plays, 80 yards in 5:37.
FALCONS: Kroy Biermann 4-yard fumble return (Elam kick).

2ND
SAINTS: Marques Colston 18-yard pass from Drew Brees (Carney kick). Twelve plays, 80 yards in 6:36.
SAINTS: Reggie Bush 1-yard run (Carney kick). Six plays, 80 yards in 1:41.
SAINTS: Jabari Greer 48-yard interception return (Carney kick).

3RD
FALCONS: Roddy White 68-yard pass from Matt Ryan (Elam kick). Three plays, 68 yards in 1:26.

4TH
FALCONS: Elam 25-yard field goal. Fourteen plays, 70 yards in 6:45.
SAINTS: Thomas 1-yard pass from Brees (Carney kick). Eleven plays, 81 yards in 5:27.
FALCONS: Elam 40-yard field goal. Seven plays, 31 yards in 55 seconds.

TEAM STATISTICS

	SAINTS	FALCONS
FIRST DOWNS	23	21
TOTAL OFFENSIVE PLAYS-YARDS (NET)	70-437	69-442
RUSHES-YARDS (NET)	35-146	24-161
PASSING YARDS (NET)	291	281
PASSES (COMP-ATT-INT)	25-33-1	19-42-3
PUNTS (NUMBER-AVG)	2-44.5	3-38.7
PUNT RETURNS-YARDS	3-88	6-148
KICKOFF RETURNS-YARDS	3-66	1-0
PENALTY YARDS	7-65	4-25
FUMBLES-LOST	3-3	0-0
TIME OF POSSESSION	33:14	26:46
FIELD GOALS (ATT-MADE)	1-0	4-2

kept slamming the door shut each time it was cracked open, providing just as many heroics as the Saints' high-powered offense.

Some of the highlights included:

▶ Cornerback Jabari Greer slicing through Atlanta for a 48-yard interception return for a touchdown shortly before halftime.

▶ Cornerback Tracy Porter adding a touchdown-saving interception early in the fourth quarter, bringing in a ball tipped by linebacker Jonathan Vilma.

▶ Safety Darren Sharper reeling in the Falcons' final desperate Hail Mary attempt in the closing seconds after Atlanta made things interesting by recovering an onside kick after a field goal.

"(Porter's interception) was huge," Sharper said. "That had to be the play of the game. To get that interception and not let them get any points was huge. That's what we've been doing all year."

The Saints' defense had 21 takeaways this season, and it had scored six touchdowns. Five interceptions were returned for scores, matching the franchise record set in 1998.

New Orleans' offense against the Falcons was plenty explosive, too, with Brees throwing for 308 yards and two touchdowns, Pierre Thomas running for 91 yards and scoring twice, and receivers Marques Colston, Jeremy Shockey, Devery Henderson and Robert Meachem making a series of spectacular catches.

But the performance was bittersweet for a unit that turned the ball over four times — an interception and three fumbles, one of which was returned for a touchdown in the first quarter.

"We did a lot of things well, yet we did a lot of things that made it close in the end," Payton said. "We've got some ball security issues, but third down was a good down for us on both sides of the ball. I thought we operated well in the red zone, and I thought we came up big on defense after (those turnovers).

"I'm excited to win, though. I'm excited to win this game and get to 7-0. It was an important win against a divisional opponent."

Said Brees when asked if he was concerned about New Orleans peaking too early: "I'll be honest, I don't think we played that great today. I think our best is yet to come. Obviously, the defense is playing great. They're doing a great job of taking the ball away, giving us opportunities on offense. Our scoring defense has been unbelievable. They're scoring plenty of touchdowns on their own.

"There's a bunch of ways to win in this league, and we've encountered a few of those ways already — and I'm sure there will be more to come."

MICHAEL DeMOCKER / THE TIMES-PICAYUNE

The fortunes of New Orleans and receiver Marques Colston didn't come crashing down against Atlanta.

SAINTS | PANTHERS

30

20

Saints defensive lineman Anthony Hargrove and his teammates don't
need the referee to make this call. Touchdown!

MATTHEW HINTON / THE TIMES-PICAYUNE

SUPER SAINTS

54

New Orleans running back Reggie Bush tries to gather steam with Carolina in hot pursuit.

MICHAEL DeMOCKER / THE TIMES-PICAYUNE

SAINTS | PANTHERS
30   20

'CRAZY' EIGHTH

New Orleans bounces back from a shaky start to turn back Carolina and go 8-0 for the first time in franchise history

By Brian Allee-Walsh Staff writer

With 11:19 remaining and the score tied at 20 at the Superdome, Saints quarterback Drew Brees stood in the Girod Street end zone, head down, away from his five offensive linemen who hovered nearby.

It was hats off to the Saints' defense as Carolina Panthers running back Tyrell Sutton was stacked up during the fourth quarter of New Orleans' 30-20 victory. After falling behind early by two touchdowns, the defense allowed six points in the final three quarters.

On the Saints' sideline, Coach Sean Payton huddled with wide receivers Marques Colston and Devery Henderson, tight end David Thomas and running backs Reggie Bush and Pierre Thomas.

Ninety-eight yards and the begrudging Panthers stood between the Saints and a go-ahead score.

"We all knew what we had to do," running back Pierre Thomas said. "We said, 'Let's take it 98 yards, let's take it all the way and keep this thing going.'"

New Orleans fell short of its goal, but "this thing," as Thomas called it, was alive and kicking.

The Black & Gold drove 76 yards to Carolina's 22-yard line, where John Carney kicked a 40-yard field goal for a 23-20 lead with 4:36 remaining. A few minutes later, defensive tackle Anthony Hargrove put the game out of reach with a 1-yard scoop-and-score on a recovered fumble en route to a come-from-behind victory before a deafening sellout crowd of 70,011.

New Orleans improved to 8-0 and stayed a game ahead of the Minnesota Vikings (7-1) in the race for home-field advantage during the playoffs in the NFC.

In the process, the Saints established a franchise benchmark with an 8-0 start, besting the 7-0 start by the 1991 team under Coach Jim Mora.

"Man, 1991 is a long time ago," Hargrove said. "I was 8 years old, in foster care in Queens (N.Y.)."

And it had the potential to get crazier and crazier with road games against the St. Louis Rams (1-7) and Tampa

PANTHERS	1ST 14	2ND 3	3RD 3	4TH 0	F 20
SAINTS	0	6	14	10	30

8-0

RECORD AFTER GAME 8

INDIVIDUAL STATISTICS

RUSHING

SAINTS: Pierre Thomas 13-50, Mike Bell 5-17.
PANTHERS: DeAngelo Williams 21-149, Jonathan Stewart 13-24.

PASSING

SAINTS: Drew Brees 24-35-330-1-1.
PANTHERS: Jake Delhomme 17-30-201-0-0.

RECEIVING

SAINTS: Reggie Bush 7-37, Robert Meachem 5-98.
PANTHERS: Steve Smith 4-64, Dwayne Jarrett 4-30.

INTERCEPTIONS

SAINTS: none.
PANTHERS: Chris Gamble 1.

SACKS

SAINTS: Will Smith 2.
PANTHERS: Tyler Brayton 1.

TACKLES (unassisted)

SAINTS: Roman Harper 10, Jonathan Vilma 10.
PANTHERS: Jon Beason 11, Chris Gamble 6.

Ouch! Panthers running back Tyrell Sutton is stopped in his tracks by a swarming Saints defense.

SCOTT THRELKELD / THE TIMES-PICAYUNE

SCORING SUMMARY

1ST
PANTHERS: DeAngelo Williams 66-yard run (John Kasay kick). Two plays, 75 yards in one minute.
PANTHERS: Williams 7-yard run (Kasay kick). Two plays, 11 yards in 46 seconds.

2ND
SAINTS: John Carney 23-yard field goal. Fifteen plays, 74 yards in 8:12.
PANTHERS: Kasay 32-yard field goal. Ten plays, 41 yards in 5:26.
SAINTS: Carney 25-yard field goal. Eleven plays, 76 yards in 1:39.

3RD
SAINTS: Pierre Thomas 10-yard run (Carney kick). Four plays, 80 yards in 1:46.
PANTHERS: Kasay 25-yard field goal. Nineteen plays, 73 yards in 9:47.
SAINTS: Robert Meachem 54-yard pass from Drew Brees (Carney kick). Six plays, 73 yards in 3:27.

4TH
SAINTS: Carney 40-yard field goal. Thirteen plays, 76 yards in 6:43.
SAINTS: Anthony Hargrove 1-yard fumble return (Carney kick).

TEAM STATISTICS

	SAINTS	PANTHERS
FIRST DOWNS	18	21
TOTAL OFFENSIVE PLAYS-YARDS (NET)	59-414	71-371
RUSHES-YARDS (NET)	23-84	39-182
PASSING YARDS (NET)	330	189
PASSES (COMP-ATT-INT)	24-35-1	17-30-0
PUNTS (NUMBER-AVG)	3-38.7	3-37.3
PUNT RETURNS-YARDS	1-4	0-0
KICKOFF RETURNS-YARDS	3-65	5-97
PENALTY YARDS	7-55	6-37
FUMBLES-LOST	2-1	5-3
TIME OF POSSESSION	27:34	32:26
FIELD GOALS (ATT-MADE)	3-3	2-2

MATTHEW HINTON / THE TIMES-PICAYUNE

Quarterback Drew Brees finds the going tough, despite completing 24 of 35 passes for 330 yards.

Bay Buccaneers (1-7) the next two weeks.

For those keeping score, back to back wins against the Buccaneers and Rams would make the Saints 10-0 going into their nationally televised "Monday Night Football" encounter against the New England Patriots on Nov. 30 at the Superdome.

Crazy?

"Eight-and-0 is nice, but we'd rather go for the big 19-0," New Orleans free safety Darren Sharper said. "That is our ultimate goal."

Said Saints defensive end Will Smith: "Going 16-0 and finishing the regular season would be great, but we want to win the (NFC South) division and get home-field advantage. The only thing this win today guarantees us is 8-8. That's all."

Unlike the Saints' first five victories — games in which they never trailed — the victory against Carolina was in doubt from the outset.

The Panthers racked up two touchdowns in the first eight minutes and seven seconds, thanks to scoring runs of 66 and 7 yards by DeAngelo Williams, a punishing scatback who finished with 149 yards on 21 carries.

Carolina finished with 182 yards rushing, but 86 in the final three quarters.

"We weren't overconfident by any stretch," Panthers Coach John Fox said. "We played this team before, and we know their potency on offense. It's a 60-minute game."

In the second quarter, Carolina sandwiched a 32-yard field goal by John Kasay between field goals of 23 and 25 yards by John Carney, leaving New Orleans trailing 17-6 at halftime.

Ten of the Panthers' points were the result of two Brees turnovers — a fumble at New Orleans' 11 and an interception by cornerback Chris Gamble at the Panthers' 4.

Those mistakes might have hurt past Saints teams but not this season's team.

"I take responsibility for the way we came out offensively," said Brees, who completed 24 of 35 passes for 330 yards, with one touchdown and one interception for a 96.1 passer rating. "I turned the ball over twice. I'm really disappointed in myself, knowing how important the game was today."

The Saints blanked Carolina 10-0 in the final 15 minutes, leaving Payton to put his team's 8-0 start in perspective.

"There hasn't been a rich history here," said Payton, while acknowledging the number of good teams under Mora during his 10 1/2 year tenure. "But (8-0) doesn't really promise you anything.

"I am encouraged with how we've been playing. I'm encouraged that we've been able to win some games without playing our best football."

SUPER SAINTS

59

SAINTS | RAMS
28 | 23

The Rams can only watch as the Saints' Reggie Bush finds the end zone in the second quarter.
BRETT DUKE / THE TIMES-PICAYUNE

SUPER SAINTS

61

SAINTS | BUCCANEERS

38 7

New Orleans linebacker Scott Fujita has a firm grasp
of the situation, sacking Tampa Bay's Josh Freeman.

CHRIS GRANGER / THE TIMES-PICAYUNE

SUPER SAINTS

65

SAINTS | BUCCANEERS
38   7

HANGING 10

In dominating fashion,
New Orleans comes out of
its funk against Tampa Bay,
rides wave of optimism

By Mike Triplett Staff writer

The hype had begun.

Actually, the buildup to a "Monday Night Football" showdown against the New England Patriots at the Superdome in eight days started when the Saints' schedule came out in April.

But now that New Orleans had dispensed with its first 10 opponents — the latest an overwhelmed Tampa Bay Buccaneers squad in a 38-7 rout in Tampa, Fla. — the anticipation was reaching a fever pitch.

"Everyone's going to blow this game up to be the biggest thing in the world," Saints linebacker Scott Fujita said. "We've just got to keep our composure and not let anything affect us, not have any distractions and just follow the mindset we've had all year."

Momentum and confidence wasn't a problem for New Orleans since it had won every game this season, but especially because of the way they played against the Buccaneers.

After a four-week stretch of sloppy performances, the Saints ran away with an efficient and thorough victory over Tampa Bay (1-9).

"We needed a game like this to come out, to look sharp in all phases," said New Orleans quarterback Drew Brees, who threw for 187 yards and three touchdowns, with no interceptions.

The Saints started slow on offense and trailed 7-0 after allowing a 95-yard touchdown drive. But the Buccaneers didn't show any more signs of life, as New Orleans won the turnover battle (4-0) and didn't allow a sack.

"It wasn't always pretty," Brees said. "The first half, (we were) one of six on third downs. . . . Then, obviously, we broke the seal there in the second half and came out with a lot of points.

"If you look at us historically, especially this year — if we take care of the football and eliminate negative plays — we are very, very hard to beat. And, obviously, when the defense is taking the ball away like they did today and have been, it gives us so many more opportunities."

The most impressive part of New Orleans' defensive dominance was that it was so depleted by injuries.

The Saints were without starting defensive tackle Sedrick Ellis and starting cornerbacks Jabari Greer and Tracy Porter. They also kept new cornerback Chris McAlister on the bench, deciding that he was not quite in football shape. During the game, cornerbacks Randall Gay and Leigh Torrence were injured, causing New Orleans to use backup safety Usama Young as an emergency cornerback.

"We are having a little bad luck curse right now, a little funk," said Gay, who suffered a hamstring injury in the second quarter and did not return. "But it shows the character and that the next guy has to step up. Hey, seven points (allowed). With four cornerbacks out, that's huge."

Rookie cornerback Malcolm Jenkins, in particular, stood out in his first NFL start. He held up all game, but the highlight was a terrific athletic play to snag his first career interception in the second quarter when the score was tied at 7.

Jenkins changed direction and dived back to his left to make the catch after receiver Antonio Bryant ran one way and Tampa Bay rookie quarterback Josh Freeman threw the other way.

"I jumped it, and when I jumped it (Bryant) kind of just broke off his route because I kind of cut him off," Jenkins said.

Freeman, who was making his third career start, looked good on the first drive, using his legs and his powerful arm to convert three third downs, including an 18-yard touchdown strike to receiver Michael Clayton in the back of the end zone.

Freeman had a lot of time to throw on the play, and the Saints' makeshift secondary had communication problems, leaving Clayton wide open.

After that, though, the Saints' pass rush improved, and defensive coordinator Gregg Williams flummoxed Freeman with a variety of blitzes and alignments.

Brees said New Orleans hadn't really accomplished anything yet, and he didn't believe the Saints had reached their peak.

"I feel like the sky's the limit for this team," Brees said. "But it's only going to get harder. Every team that

Saints defensive end Will Smith (91) sacks the
Buccaneers' Josh Freeman, and defensive end
Charles Grant piles on.
CHRIS GRANGER / THE TIMES-PICAYUNE

SUPER SAINTS

67

BUCS	1ST 7	2ND 0	3RD 0	4TH 0	F 7
SAINTS	7	10	14	7	38

RECORD AFTER GAME 10

SCORING SUMMARY

1ST **BUCCANEERS:** Michael Clayton 18-yard pass from Josh Freeman (Connor Barth kick). Twelve plays, 95 yards in 6:55.
SAINTS: Robert Meachem 4-yard pass from Drew Brees (John Carney kick). Seven plays, 68 yards in 3:54.

2ND **SAINTS:** Carney 38-yard field goal. Four plays, 9 yards in 1:17.
SAINTS: Meachem 6-yard pass from Brees (Carney kick). Five plays, 63 yards in 1:10.

3RD **SAINTS:** David Thomas 11-yard pass from Brees (Carney kick). Three plays, 15 yards in 1:25.
SAINTS: Mike Bell 3-yard run (Carney kick). Six plays, 55 yards in 2:10.

4TH **SAINTS:** Bell 1-yard run (Carney kick). Thirteen plays, 82 yards in 7:26.

INDIVIDUAL STATISTICS

RUSHING

SAINTS: Pierre Thomas 11-92, Mike Bell 13-75.
BUCCANEERS: Carnell Williams 11-32, Earnest Graham 3-31.

PASSING

SAINTS: Drew Brees 19-29-187-3-0.
BUCCANEERS: Josh Freeman 17-33-126-1-3.

RECEIVING

SAINTS: Marques Colston 5-74, David Thomas 4-66.
BUCCANEERS: Kellen Winslow 5-29, Antonio Bryant 3-40.

TEAM STATISTICS

	SAINTS	BUCS
FIRST DOWNS	21	14
TOTAL OFFENSIVE PLAYS-YARDS (NET)	65-370	59-219
RUSHES-YARDS (NET)	36-183	23-119
PASSING YARDS (NET)	187	100
PASSES (COMP-ATT-INT)	19-29-0	17-33-3
PUNTS (NUMBER-AVG)	4-44.8	5-41.2
PUNT RETURNS-YARDS	3-16	1-11
KICKOFF RETURNS-YARDS	2-51	4-106
PENALTY YARDS	4-55	3-18
FUMBLES-LOST	0-0	1-1
TIME OF POSSESSION	32:24	27:36
FIELD GOALS (ATT-MADE)	1-1	0-0

CHRIS GRANGER / THE TIMES-PICAYUNE

Saints tight end David Thomas is congratulated following his 11-yard touchdown reception from quarterback Drew Brees.

INTERCEPTIONS

SAINTS: Malcolm Jenkins 1, Chris Reis 1, Jonathan Vilma 1.
BUCCANEERS: none.

SACKS

SAINTS: Scott Fujita 1, Will Smith 1, Roman Harper 0.5, Leigh Torrence 0.5
BUCCANEERS: none.

TACKLES (unassisted)

SAINTS: Jonathan Vilma 6, Malcolm Jenkins 5.
BUCCANEERS: Bo Rudd 8, Ronde Barber 6.

CHRIS GRANGER / THE TIMES-PICAYUNE
Receiver Robert Meachem scored twice on touchdown receptions (4 and 6 yards) against the Buccaneers.

we play would love to be the team to give us that first loss. And we're about to play a team who arguably has been one of the best teams in this league the last decade, somewhat of a dynasty. They know how to win; they know how to win big games. And obviously we want to be one of those teams, year in and year out that's fighting for a championship.

"We're building something special right now, but we also have to understand that in order to get there, you've got to be able to win games like this one coming up."

SAINTS | PATRIOTS

38

17

Saints receiver Devery Henderson, who had three catches for 116 yards, grasps the situation.

ELIOT KAMENITZ / THE TIMES-PICAYUNE

New Orleans receiver
Robert Meachem
catches in stride a
38-yard touchdown pass
in the second quarter.

CHUCK COOK / THE TIMES-PICAYUNE

SAINTS | PATRIOTS
38   17

PAT ON THE BACK

The Saints turn heads in a big way and move to 11-0 with their dismantling of the Patriots in prime time

By Nakia Hogan Staff writer

Did Saints fans believe?

If they hadn't, it now was time to start, especially after what happened in front of 70,768 fans at a sold-out Superdome and before millions more on "Monday Night Football."

Despite roaring to a franchise-record 10 consecutive victories to the open the season, there still was some questions about the validity of New Orleans and its star quarterback Drew Brees.

No more.

Brees passed for five touchdowns as the Saints scored an emphatic 38-17 victory over the New England Patriots.

"It does (validate the Saints) in the public's eye," New Orleans safety Darren Sharper said, "because everyone still believes in the Patriots, and they are one of the best teams in the NFL — and everyone thought they were going to come in here and knock us off. We took that as a challenge and motivation."

The Saints (11-0) could wrap up their second NFC South title since Coach Sean Payton arrived in New Orleans in 2006 with a victory at Washington in six days or a loss by the Atlanta Falcons, who were set to host the Philadelphia Eagles.

But the Saints were playing for much more than just a division title.

It was clear that New Orleans, one of two remaining unbeaten teams along with the Indianapolis Colts, were among a handful of teams with a legitimate shot to reach Super Bowl XLIV on Feb. 7 in Miami.

Throughout the week leading to the game, Patriots Coach Bill Belichick said as much, but his words were downplayed as gamesmanship and a bit of subterfuge.

"People are going to talk about this game and blow it out of proportion a little bit, but this game doesn't entitle us to anything," Brees said. "It's just another win in the win column.

No keeping this a secret: The Drew Brees to Marques Colston connection yields another touchdown.

TED JACKSON / THE TIMES-PICAYUNE

Defensive end Bobby McCray gives New England quarterback Tom Brady no room to back up on 'Monday Night Football.'

"It only counts for one win on the stat sheet, but emotionally these types of wins can mean a little bit more. We played tremendous football tonight."

Brees, who outplayed counterpart Tom Brady of the Patriots (7-4), was dominant from the outset. He completed 18 of 23 passes for a season-high 371 yards, with five touchdowns and no interceptions on his way to his first career perfect quarterback rating of 158.3. He was the first quarterback to throw five scoring passes against a Belichick defense.

Brees guided the Saints to scores on six of their 11 possessions. All five of his touchdown passes went to different receivers, and New Orleans averaged a franchise-record 9.6 yards per play.

Marques Colston led the receivers with four catches for 121 yards and a touchdown, and Devery Henderson caught three passes for 116 yards and a touchdown.

"The crazy thing is, that's what this offense is like," Colston said.

Brees was as calm and accurate in the pocket as ever, but much of the credit for this victory had to go to the Saints' banged-up cornerback group.

With starting cornerbacks Tracy Porter (knee) and Jabari Greer (groin) missing the game because of injuries and No. 3 cornerback Randall Gay leaving on the first possession after aggravating his hamstring injury, New Orleans managed to slow the Patriots' passing attack with rookie Malcolm Jenkins and two newly acquired

veterans — Mike McKenzie and Chris McAlister.

Brady didn't appear to find his rhythm against the Saints' secondary. He completed 21 of 36 passes for 237 yards, but he threw two interceptions and no touchdowns.

The first interception — by McKenzie, who was playing in his first game since Nov. 9, 2008 — set up New Orleans' first touchdown.

"Obviously, this is a big win for us to get our 11th win," Payton said. "I thought we played a complementary game. I thought defensively with the injuries, we did a good job. With the depth at corner, some new guys really stepped up."

Perhaps the biggest momentum swing came late in the third quarter with New England threatening to cut into the Saints' 31-17 lead. On a fourth-and-4 at New Orleans' 10-yard line, McKenzie broke up a pass intended for receiver Randy Moss — all but killing any opportunity for a Patriots' comeback.

"It was no doubt that we needed some points at that point," said Belichick, whose team was 2-for-3 on fourth-down attempts. "I thought we were running the game well at that point offensively. I thought we needed more than a field goal the way the game was going. McKenzie made a good play over there."

Said Saints defensive end Will Smith: "This wasn't the Super Bowl nor was it a playoff game. It was just a regular-season game. Fortunately, we came out with the win."

PATRIOTS	1ST 7	2ND 3	3RD 7	4TH 0	F 17
SAINTS	3	21	7	7	38

11-0

RECORD AFTER GAME 11

Robert Meachum

INDIVIDUAL STATISTICS

RUSHING
SAINTS: Pierre Thomas 11-64, Mike Bell 13-50.
PATRIOTS: Laurence Maroney 15-64, Kevin Faulk 3-22.

PASSING
SAINTS: Drew Brees 18-23-371-5-0.
PATRIOTS: Tom Brady 21-36-237-0-2, Brian Hoyer 2-4-19-0-0.

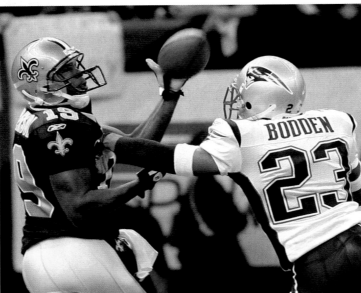

TED JACKSON / THE TIMES-PICAYUNE

New Orleans receiver Devery Henderson finds some space against the Patriots.

RECEIVING
SAINTS: Robert Meachem 5-69, Marques Colston 4-121.
PATRIOTS: Sam Aiken 7-90, Wes Welker 6-32.

INTERCEPTIONS
SAINTS: Mike McKenzie 1, Darren Sharper 1.
PATRIOTS: none.

SACKS
SAINTS: Will Smith 1.5, Bobby McCray 0.5.
PATRIOTS: Adalius Thomas 1.

TACKLES (unassisted)
SAINTS: Jonathan Vilma 8, Roman Harper 5.
PATRIOTS: Braydon Meriweather 6, Gary Guyton 6.

GAME STATISTICS
Attendance: 70,768 at Superdome

SCORING SUMMARY

1ST
SAINTS: John Carney 30-yard field goal. Eight plays, 53 yards in 3:46.
PATRIOTS: Laurence Maroney 4-yard run (Stephen Gostkowski kick). Fourteen plays, 80 yards in 7:40.

2ND
SAINTS: Pierre Thomas 18-yard pass from Drew Brees (Carney kick). Seven plays, 59 yards in 3:07.
SAINTS: Devery Henderson 75-yard pass from Brees (Carney kick). One play, 75 yards in nine seconds.
PATRIOTS: Gostkowski 36-yard field goal. Eleven plays, 58 yards in 5:39.
SAINTS: Robert Meachem 38-yard pass from Brees (Carney kick). Five plays, 76 yards in 2:24.

3RD
PATRIOTS: Maroney 2-yard run (Gostkowski kick). Eight plays, 81 yards in 4:16.
SAINTS: Darnell Dinkins 2-yard pass from Brees (Carney kick). Three plays, 74 yards in 1:22.

4TH
SAINTS: Marques Colston 20-yard pass from Brees Carney kick). Nine plays, 75 yards in 5:18.

TEAM STATISTICS

	SAINTS	PATRIOTS
FIRST DOWNS	18	23
TOTAL OFFENSIVE PLAYS-YARDS (NET)	50-480	70-366
RUSHES-YARDS (NET)	26-113	28-122
PASSING YARDS (NET)	367	244
PASSES (COMP-ATT-INT)	18-23-0	23-40-2
PUNTS (NUMBER-AVG)	3-43.3	3-46.0
PUNT RETURNS-YARDS	2-6	1-41
KICKOFF RETURNS-YARDS	4-95	3-80
PENALTY YARDS	4-36	0-0
FUMBLES-LOST	1-1	2-1
TIME OF POSSESSION	26:44	33:16
FIELD GOALS (ATT-MADE)	2-1	2-1

Saints receiver Robert Meachem had five catches for 69 yards, including a 38-yard touchdown reception.

TED JACKSON / THE TIMES-PICAYUNE

SUPER SAINTS

SAINTS | PATRIOTS
38   17

Mike McKenzie's return is memorable, and he steps up just like a champ

JOHN DESHAZIER

Of all the improbable, unlikely and utterly unbelievable twists and turns that had accompanied the Saints' magically perfect 2009 season, a singular spotlight now was reserved for cornerback Mike McKenzie.

Make that a nationally televised "Monday Night Football" spotlight, when New Orleans marched to 11-0 with a 38-17 victory over New England that should've included a warning for viewers, given that the Saints casually undressed the Patriots and left them bare at the Superdome.

McKenzie joined the season-long party and scripted his signature against no less a team than the Patriots and no less a receiver than Randy Moss. Yes, that Randy Moss, whose freakish playmaking skills had left a trail of frustrated, muttering, beaten cornerbacks in his wake during 12 Hall of Fame-caliber seasons in the NFL.

"He did a good job," Saints Coach Sean Payton said, which was about the equivalent of saying New Orleans was fairly adequate this season.

Any rational mind thought Saints fans had seen the last of McKenzie on March 19, 2009, when he was released by the franchise. In Week 10 of the 2008 season he broke his right kneecap — the same knee that had undergone surgery for a torn ACL in the 2007 season.

And since the market wasn't a robust one for 33-year-old cornerbacks with two significant injuries to the same knee in consecutive seasons, it wasn't unreasonable to assume the last vision of McKenzie in a Saints uniform was of him being carted off the field at the Georgia Dome in Atlanta.

But against New England, he turned in a virtuoso defensive performance in front of the 70,768 fans that comprised the second-largest crowd in Superdome history but staked its claim as the loudest.

"This group is very special," McKenzie said. "I feel honored just to have the opportunity to go out there and play with these guys. If we go out there and keep working, good things are going to happen to us."

McKenzie, who hadn't played an NFL game since Nov. 9, 2008, and who was signed all of one week before facing Moss and the Patriots, played lock-down corner like he had a point to prove.

And points to help prevent.

He virtually climbed inside Moss' jersey, and anyone else New England sent his way, and draped them like sweat, becoming a major piece of a revamped Saints secondary that was missing injured starting cornerbacks Jabari Greer and Tracy Porter, and that had lost Randall Gay, who started against New England, to an injury in the first quarter.

Three solo tackles, three passes defensed and one monumental, momentum-changing interception was not the kind of work expected of a player who hadn't lined up against a receiver this season. It wasn't expected of a player who had spent more time in the Superdome suites than on anyone's field.

But in this magnificent season of the Saints, improbable, unlikely and unbelievable all had ceded control to New Orleans' golden touch.

McKenzie wore the magic gloves against the Patriots, and he put them to use in the first quarter.

Of course, he had help from a teammate. Because if receiver Courtney Roby hadn't run down New England's Wes Welker from behind on Welker's 41-yard punt return, it would've been an 87-yard return for a touchdown, a 14-3 Patriots lead and another deep, early deficit for the Saints.

But because Roby made his play, and the Patriots set up first-and-10 at the Saints' 46-yard line, McKenzie was able to do his thing.

Which was this: Intercept New England quarterback Tom Brady on first down, on a pass intended for Moss, and return it 8 yards to the Saints' 41 with 1:02 remaining in the quarter.

The 14-point swing was completed 3:07 later, with 12:55 remaining in the second quarter, when quarterback Drew Brees threw the first of his five touchdown passes for the Saints, an 18-yarder to running back Pierre Thomas, which gave New Orleans a 10-7 lead it never relinquished.

"The interception was a big play," Payton said. "Mike kind of undercut the throw that was headed for Moss. We ended up scoring on that possession."

McKenzie ended up scoring points with his team-

TED JACKSON / THE TIMES-PICAYUNE

Newly signed cornerback Mike McKenzie doesn't waste any time, snagging a pass intended for Patriots receiver Randy Moss.

mates.

"That's what you get from veteran corners," Brees said of McKenzie and Chris McAlister, another formerly injured, veteran cornerback who joined New Orleans six days before McKenzie. "They've played a lot; they've seen a lot."

But neither had seen a Saints team like this one, capable of scoring 21 points in the second quarter, on drives of 59, 75 and 76 yards, totaling a minuscule five minutes, 40 seconds.

And neither had played with a quarterback like Brees, who, fittingly, had a perfect passer rating (158.3) while completing 18 of 23 passes for 371 yards and his

five touchdowns.

"I thought he was magnificent," Payton said.

So, too, was McKenzie, whose final big play was a near-interception — of another pass intended for Moss — on fourth-and-4 from the Saints' 10 with 4:12 remaining in the third quarter.

"McKenzie made a good play over there," Patriots Coach Bill Belichick said.

Said Payton: "Some new guys really stepped up and handled their role well."

Especially McKenzie, the latest improbable, unlikely, unbelievable hero for the Saints in what was a growing line of them this season.

SAINTS | REDSKINS OT

33 **30**

Saints Coach Sean Payton
has a great view as
receiver Robert Meachem
returns a fumble 44 yards
for a touchdown.
JOHN McCUSKER / THE TIMES-PICAYUNE

SUPER SAINTS

The Saints knew they were back in business when Shaun Suisham missed a 23-yard field-goal attempt late in the fourth quarter.

MICHAEL DeMOCKER / THE TIMES-PICAYUNE

SAINTS | REDSKINS OT

33   30

'UNBELIEVABLE' 12TH

New Orleans captures NFC South title by getting some late breaks to defeat Washington in overtime and stay unbeaten

By Mike Triplett Staff writer

The word "destiny" was floating around quite a bit in the Saints' locker room after their improbable 33-30 victory in overtime against the Washington Redskins in Landover, Md., and a few players admitted that sometimes "it's better to be lucky than good."

Coach Sean Payton wasn't about to credit any mystical forces after New Orleans rallied from 10 points down in the final seven minutes for its most dramatic victory of the season. In the process, the Saints clinched the NFC South title and pushed their record to 12-0.

"I don't think it works like that," Payton said when asked if New Orleans could credit luck or divine intervention for its latest escape. "I don't believe in that; I believe you've got to make your own way each week.

"Look, when you do this long enough, you find yourself on the end of wins maybe sometimes that you feel fortunate to have, and you find yourself in losses that you feel like maybe shouldn't have happened. That's just how this game is, and you've just got to keep playing.

"This team didn't quit, and I'm proud of 'em. . . . It was an exciting win. It was unbelievable."

The Saints knew better than most NFL franchises about living with the agony of such defeats. Last season, in particular, they made a monthly ritual of finding new and creative ways to cough up games in the final minutes — one of them at the very same FedExField.

But whether it was divine intervention, a newfound confidence, a higher level of performance or some magical combination of all three, these weren't the same old Saints.

"To beat us, you have to play a full game," New Orleans right tackle Jon Stinchcomb.

Also, the Saints got some breathing room in the race to have home-field advantage throughout the playoffs.

REDSKINS	1ST 10	2ND 7	3RD 10	4TH 3	OT 0	F 30
SAINTS	0	17	3	10	3	33

Jonathan Casillas

12-0

RECORD AFTER GAME 12

INDIVIDUAL STATISTICS

RUSHING

SAINTS: Mike Bell 16-34, Pierre Thomas 6-18.
REDSKINS: Quinton Ganther 8-46, Rock Cartwright 13-39.

PASSING

SAINTS: Drew Brees 35-49-419-2-1.
REDSKINS: Jason Campbell 30-42-367-3-1.

RECEIVING

SAINTS: Robert Meachem 8-142, Pierre Thomas 8-64.
REDSKINS: Devin Thomas 7-100, Santana Moss 5-68.

MICHAEL DeMOCKER / THE TIMES-PICAYUNE

In overtime, cornerback Chris McAlister' hit against Redskins fullback Mike Sellers produces a turnover.

INTERCEPTIONS

SAINTS: Jonathan Vilma 1.
REDSKINS: Dareem Moore 1.

SACKS

SAINTS: none.
REDSKINS: LaRon Landry 1.

TACKLES (unassisted)

SAINTS: Malcolm Jenkins 8, Sedrick Ellis 6.
REDSKINS: LaRon Landry 12, Rocky McIntosh 6.

GAME STATISTICS
Attendance: 84,520 at FedExField

SCORING SUMMARY

1ST
REDSKINS: Fred Davis 8-yard pass from Jason Campbell (Shaun Suisham kick). Nine plays, 94 yards in 4:40.
REDSKINS: Suisham 32-yard field goal. Nine plays, 57 yards in 3:29.

2ND
SAINTS: Garrett Hartley 34-yard field goal. Twelve plays, 50 yards in 5:34.
SAINTS: Marques Colston 40-yard pass from Drew Brees (Hartley kick). Nine plays, 87 yards in 4:27.
REDSKINS: Devin Thomas 5-yard pass from Campbell. Nine plays, 78 yards in 3:17.
SAINTS: Robert Meachem 44-yard fumble return (Hartley kick).

3RD
REDSKINS: Suisham 28-yard field goal. Ten plays, 64 yards in four minutes.
REDSKINS: Thomas 13-yard pass from Campbell (Suisham kick). Four plays, 56 yards in 1:34.
SAINTS: Hartley 27-yard field goal. Ten plays, 64 yards in 5:13.

4TH
REDSKINS: Suisham 21-yard field goal. Nine plays, 63 yards in 4:44.
SAINTS: Hartley 28-yard field goal. Twelve plays, 69 yards in 5:59.
SAINTS: Meachem 53-yard pass from Brees (Hartley kick). Five plays, 80 yards in 33 seconds.

OT
SAINTS: Hartley 18-yard field goal. Eight plays, 36 yards in 5:16.

TEAM STATISTICS

	SAINTS	REDSKINS
FIRST DOWNS	25	28
TOTAL OFFENSIVE PLAYS-YARDS (NET)	74-463	67-455
RUSHES-YARDS (NET)	24-55	25-88
PASSING YARDS (NET)	408	367
PASSES (COMP-ATT-INT)	35-49-1	30-42-1
PUNTS (NUMBER-AVG)	3-33.3	1-51.0
PUNT RETURNS-YARDS	1-2	1-0
KICKOFF RETURNS-YARDS	7-145	8-177
PENALTY YARDS	7-102	2-15
FUMBLES-LOST	1-0	3-3
TIME OF POSSESSION	35:06	31:23
FIELD GOALS (ATT-MADE)	5-4	4-3

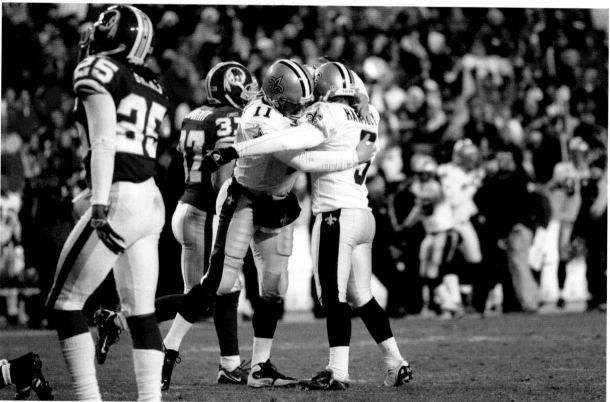

MICHAEL DeMOCKER / THE TIMES-PICAYUNE

Saints kicker Garrett Hartley, right, and holder Mark Brunell rejoice following Hartley's 18-yard field goal in overtime.

The Arizona Cardinals (8-4) defeated visiting Minnesota 30-17 later that night, dropping the Vikings to 10-2.

The Saints rallied from a 30-20 deficit in the final seven minutes of regulation against the Redskins, thanks to a 28-yard field goal by Garrett Hartley, a stunning 23-yard field-goal miss by Washington's Shaun Suisham and a vintage 53-yard touchdown pass from Drew Brees to wide receiver Robert Meachem.

An interception by New Orleans linebacker Jonathan Vilma nearly led to a winning field goal in regulation, but Hartley missed a 58-yard attempt as time expired.

It didn't matter. Saints cornerback Chris McAlister followed up with a forced fumble in overtime that led to Hartley's winning 18-yard field goal.

"I definitely believe in destiny, and I believe in karma, and what goes around comes around," said Brees, who threw for 419 yards and two touchdowns, with one interception against a feisty Redskins' defense. "Plenty of times we've been on the other side of this, where it's us missing the field goal, or it's us turning the ball over, or it's us not making the stop, or the ball just not bouncing our way.

"We've been on the other end of this plenty of times, and it's heartbreaking when that happens to you. But then again, it seems like maybe we paid our dues in past years and learned about that heartbreak and learned

how to overcome that to the point where we never want to feel like that again.

"We love this feeling."

The Redskins led 10-0 in the first quarter and 17-10 with time running out in the second.

But just before halftime, a wacky play resulted in a 44-yard touchdown by Meachem.

Brees threw an interception to safety Kareem Moore on the play, but after Moore returned the ball 14 yards, Meachem caught him from behind and snatched the ball out of his hands — then returned it 44 yards for a score to tie it at 17.

Washington led 27-17 in the third quarter and 30-20 in the fourth, and the Redskins marched inside the Saints' 5-yard line with less than two minutes remaining in regulation, needing just a chip-shot field goal to put the game out of reach.

But once Suisham pushed his kick wide right, in part because of a high snap, New Orleans was convinced it had just won the game.

Suisham had never missed a kick from inside 30 yards in his career.

"You could see it in people's eyes," Saints running back Mike Bell said. "They were ready to go. We knew we were going to win once he missed that field goal."

DAVID GRUNFELD / THE TMES-PICAYUNE

Throughout the season, Saints players and coaches were given a hero's welcome at Louis Armstrong International Airport.

SIMPLY FANTASTIC!

AS THE WINS PILE UP, THE SAINTS ARE TREATED LIKE HEROES AT THE AIRPORT FOLLOWING AWAY GAMES

By Mary Sparacello Staff writer

If you were looking for more proof that Saints fans were the loudest, craziest, most intense individuals anywhere in the NFL, you needed to look no further than a half-mile stretch in Kenner.

That was where fans had gathered for years to greet the Saints as they arrived at Louis Armstrong International Airport from road games, where the Black & Gold then left in a caravan headed to Veterans Memorial Boulevard and points throughout the New Orleans area.

Six off-duty police officers handled the crowds at the start of the 2009 season, but 18 officers were needed for the growing throngs who had showed up as the regular season drew to a close, Kenner Police Chief Steve Caraway said.

As Saints players drove past them, fans (sometimes five or six deep behind barricades) — some wearing costumes — waved their arms or displayed signs, with some screaming.

"It's kind of like Mardi Gras," Caraway said.

And like Mardi Gras, it was something apparently found only in New Orleans.

"The phenomenon of being there for every game and making it an event, I've never heard of that before, " said Joe Horrigan, vice president of communications for the Pro Football Hall of Fame.

He applauded Saints fans.

"It's always great to see grass-roots phenomenons," he said.

Returning home after a New Orleans road game to crowds of fans "has become a great Saints tradition, unique among NFL teams," the team said in a statement.

With each victory this season, Caraway said, more and more fans showed up to greet home the team — and the numbers had gotten the attention of the Saints.

Quarterback Drew Brees said fans had thrown CDs, pralines and T-shirts into his car.

"It's like Christmas," he said. "I think it's great how excited people are."

In November, when New Orleans was 9-0, the team acknowledged the growing crowds. The organization released a message asking "the best fans in the NFL" not to approach the cars of Saints players and officials because it was unsafe.

The Saints hired off-duty Kenner police officers to barricade the half-mile route and ushered the players through the crowds to the interstate.

"Our priority is the safety of our players, coaches, staff and fans," said Greg Bensel, vice president of communications for the Saints.

Eddie Eubanks, 12, walked several blocks from his home to watch through a fence as Saints players departed their plane. Brees received the biggest cheers, Eubanks said.

"It's fun, but it's madness, " he said.

JENNIFER ZDON / THE TIMES-PICAYUNE

SAINTS | FALCONS

26

23

With the game hanging in the balance, New Orleans linebacker Jonathan Vilma thwarts Atlanta with an interception.

MICHAEL DeMOCKER / THE TIMES-PICAYUNE

SUPER SAINTS

89

SAINTS | FALCONS
26   23

WHEW, DAT!

Perfect Saints are far from perfect, but they clinch a first-round playoff bye with a triumph over the Falcons

By Nakia Hogan Staff writer

In the bowels of the Georgia Dome in Atlanta following his team's latest victory, Saints owner Tom Benson giddily made his way toward the locker room and interrupted Coach Sean Payton's postgame interview with an excited chant of "Woo Hoo."

With the way New Orleans was playing this season, it was easy to understand the longtime owner's excitement.

For the second consecutive week, the Saints displayed enough grit and wherewithal to come away with a close — if not improbable — win, defeating the Atlanta Falcons 26-23 before a crowd of 68,930.

The victory helped the NFC South champion Saints push their record to 13-0 and clinch a first-round bye in the playoffs. It also marked the most victories for a Saints team in franchise history and pushed their magic number to secure home-field advantage in the NFC during the playoffs to two.

"This is great for all the people of New Orleans and the state of Louisiana and all over the country because of how it's going right now," Benson said.

It didn't all go right for the Saints. But after an uninspired defensive performance for much of the game, New Orleans managed to come away with critical stops to secure the win against Atlanta.

The first was an interception by middle linebacker Jonathan Vilma, who picked off a Chris Redman pass intended for wide receiver Roddy White and returned it to the Falcons' 32-yard line with 3:53 remaining and the Saints clinging to a 26-23 lead.

New Orleans failed to capitalize on the turnover, however, as Payton elected to attempt a fake field goal on fourth-and-7 from Atlanta's 15. Backup quarterback Mark Brunell, the holder for field-goal attempts, threw an incomplete pass to reserve tight end Darnell Dinkins.

But Vilma again came through for a Saints defense

that yielded 392 yards against a Falcons team that was playing without starting quarterback Matt Ryan and running back Michael Turner.

Facing a fourth-and-2 at New Orleans' 46 with 1:18 remaining, Redman completed a short pass to Jason Snelling. Vilma swarmed in and tackled Snelling for a 1-yard gain, sealing the victory.

"We've been saying that since OTAs, put it on our shoulders at the end of the game," Vilma said. "Regardless of what happened during the game, whether we were playing lights out or weren't playing lights out, we understand that we can close these games out, we're going to get the victory. We had to go in with four minutes left; we were able to stop them then. Then we had to go again with two minutes, and we stopped them again."

Before Vilma's two big defensive stops, it appeared Atlanta would march down the field and at least tie the score at 26 — if not pull off the upset.

Throughout the game, Redman dissected the Saints' secondary. Playing for Ryan, who missed the game with a turf toe, Redman nearly outplayed counterpart Drew Brees.

New Orleans hardly rattled Redman. He completed 23 of 34 passes for 303 yards, with a touchdown and an interception — and he led the Falcons on scoring drives on five of their first six possessions.

Brees, who tied Aaron Brooks' franchise mark for career scoring passes with 120, completed 31 of 40 passes for 296 yards and three touchdowns.

But Brees and his teammates wouldn't have celebrated if not for the late-game heroics of Vilma.

Redman kept the Saints off balance, occasionally beating their blitzing scheme with a big play.

"This was a long, hard-fought battle — and nobody said it was going to be easy," Saints strong safety Roman Harper said. "But at the end of the day it doesn't matter how ugly it is as long as we get the W."

For the second consecutive game (last week New Orleans defeated host Washington 33-30 in overtime), New Orleans needed a late-game defensive stop to clinch a win.

And for the second consecutive game, Garrett Hartley provided the winning points, making a 38-yarder with 4:42 remaining.

Talk of an unbeaten season intensified. The Saints

New Orleans receiver Robert Meachem stretches out to corral a pass from quarterback Drew Brees.

MICHAEL DeMOCKER / THE TIMES-PICAYUNE

During the 2009 season, it was time to celebrate for Saints owner Tom Benson and owner/executive vice president Rita Benson LeBlanc.

DAVID GRUNFELD / THE TIMES-PICAYUNE

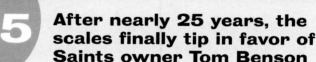

TOM BENSON

After nearly 25 years, the scales finally tip in favor of Saints owner Tom Benson

PETER FINNEY

When the Saints kicked off the 2009 regular season against the Detroit Lions on Sept. 13 at the Superdome, owner Tom Benson weighed 219 pounds.

After New Orleans defeated the Atlanta Falcons 26-23 on Dec. 13 at the Georgia Dome to improve to 13-0, he was down to 206 pounds.

"It's really sort of eerie," Benson said. "I'm on the scales once a week, and I've lost one pound a game. Now I'm on a mission."

Which was?

"I want to weigh 200 on Feb. 7 (the date of Super Bowl XLIV in Miami)," Benson said.

Picture yourself as the boss of a football team holding the Vince Lombardi Trophy, holding the silver symbol of a world champion, as you were celebrating your silver anniversary as an NFL owner.

A phone call last week reminded Benson of a nearly 25-year journey's beginning. A journey that started with his $70 million purchase of a franchise that now was valued at $942 million, according to Forbes.

"Bum Phillips had some warm words of congratulations on how the season has gone," Benson said of his first coach, someone he had inherited from a franchise owned by John Mecom Jr.

As it turned out, Phillips was Benson's coach until he resigned in 1985, handing the reins to his son, Wade, with four games remaining in what ended as a 5-11 season.

"Now you have Wade Phillips coming in (to the Superdome on) Saturday (Dec. 19) as coach of the Cowboys, looking to end our unbeaten season and keep Dallas' playoff hopes alive," Benson said. "It's going to be a war."

The ticket demand for the Cowboys game was at an all-time high, and Gov. Bobby Jindal had petitioned the NFL to see whether a game telecasted by the NFL

TOM BENSON

Network could also be televised on a broadcast channel in all of Louisiana like it was to be in New Orleans.

"It's truly amazing how Saints fever had spread," Benson said. "Shreveport, for example, because of its location, has been Dallas Cowboy territory. That's changing. I was in Dallas this week on league business. I'm in an elevator, and a lady older than me, who had no idea who I was, looks at me and says, 'Go Saints.' It's crazy."

Benson was "blown away" by the size of crowds, all ages, that had showed up at the airport to meet the Saints after road games.

"They've been well into the thousands," he said. "For road games in Tampa and Miami, ticket sales are hitting 5,000. ... We've never had as much Saints fever as we now have in Mississippi, Alabama, Texas and the Florida panhandle. That's what winning will do. It's contagious."

MATT ROSE / THE TIMES-PICAYUNE

Was Benson surprised?

"Yes and no," he said. "In March, I remember telling (General Manager) Mickey Loomis and (Coach) Sean Payton how I'd never seen such focus before by the players. When you look back on the last two seasons, we were losing toward the end of some games like we're winning games now.

"There's another thing you can't ignore. Yes, the fans have fallen in love with the players, but the players have fallen in love with the city. It works both ways. The players and the city have embraced one another. That's what makes this moment so special for everyone."

Especially for Benson, so long as he stayed away from those cones full of plain ol' vanilla.

"Yes, the fans have fallen in love with the players, but the players have fallen in love with the city. It works both ways. The players and the city have embraced one another. That's what makes this moment so special for everyone."
TOM BENSON

THOMAS MILTON BENSON JR. BORN **1927** in **New Orleans** ATTENDED **St. Aloysius, Loyola University**

SUPER SAINTS

31, 1985 Ownership of the Saints was transferred to Tom Benson for the sales price of just over $70 million.

COWBOYS | SAINTS

24 | **17**

With 12 seconds remaining, quarterback Drew Brees fumbles away the Saints' last shot against the Cowboys.

RÚSTY COSTANZA / THE TIMES-PICAYUNE

COWBOYS | SAINTS
24   17

STAR STRUCK

After winning 13 in a row, New Orleans is humbled and knocked from the ranks of the unbeaten by Dallas

By Mike Triplett Staff writer

The magic finally ran out.

The Saints nearly pulled off another miracle in the final minutes of a 24-17 loss to the Dallas Cowboys at the Superdome, but this time, when they reached into their bag of tricks, it was empty.

Their perfect season ended with quarterback Drew Brees fumbling as he fell to the turf with 10 seconds remaining after a sack by Dallas linebacker DeMarcus Ware near midfield.

"Yeah, well, that's disappointing, because you just don't know how many chances you're going to get at that — and to get as close as we did, that's tough. That's tough," said Brees, who was excited about the prospect of going undefeated in the regular season.

Not that the Saints were in bad shape, at 13-1 and still the front-runner for the No. 1 seed in the NFC playoffs. And some players even suggested the first taste of disappointment might give New Orleans even more of an edge heading into the postseason.

But clearly, they were mourning the end of their magical three-month run of perfection.

"I just felt like we fought so hard to get where we were at, and we'd won games in so many different ways, with so many guys contributing, we just felt like we deserved it," said Brees, who was uncharacteristically off-target for three quarters before stepping up to lead the Saints on two fourth-quarter touchdown drives that sent the crowd into a frenzy.

"The city deserved it, the organization deserved it, and we wanted to make it happen for them," Brees said. "That's what's most disappointing about it. But the fact is, we're 13-1 and moving forward. We understand what's on the horizon. We're just excited to get back in the field and make up for what happened today."

The Saints no longer had to worry about whether to keep pushing or rest their starters. As long as the Minnesota Vikings (11-2) kept winning, the Saints needed

COWBOYS	1ST 14	2ND 3	3RD 7	4TH 0	F 24
SAINTS	0	3	0	14	17

13-1

RECORD AFTER GAME 14

INDIVIDUAL STATISTICS

RUSHING

SAINTS: Reggie Bush 1-29, Pierre Thomas 6-20.
COWBOYS: Marion Barber 17-62, Felix Jones 14-58.

SUSAN POAG / THE TIMES-PICAYUNE

The Saints' 13–game winning streak was over. Quarterback Drew Brees and New Orleans finally tasted defeat.

PASSING

SAINTS: Drew Brees 29-45-298-1-1.
COWBOYS: Tony Romo 22-34-312-1-0.

RECEIVING

SAINTS: David Thomas 8-77, Marques Colston 5-86.
COWBOYS: Miles Austin 7-139, Jason Witten 5-44.

INTERCEPTIONS

SAINTS: none.
COWBOYS: Mike Jenkins 1.

SACKS

SAINTS: Will Smith 2, Jonathan Vilma 1.
COWBOYS: Bradie James 2, DeMarcus Ware 2.

TACKLES (unassisted)

SAINTS: Jonathan Vilma 10, Scott Fujita 9.
COWBOYS: Orlando Scandrick 7, Bradie James 6.

GAME STATISTICS
Attendance: 70,213 at Superdome

SCORING SUMMARY

1ST
COWBOYS: Miles Austin 49-yard pass from Tony Romo (Nick Folk kick). Five plays, 79 yards in 1:46.
COWBOYS: Marion Barber 3-yard run (Folk kick). Eight plays, 60 yards in 4:28.

2ND
SAINTS: Garrett Hartley 34-yard field goal. Twelve plays, 75 yards in 4:44.
COWBOYS: Folk 44-yard field goal. Five plays, minus-2 yards in 41 seconds.

3RD
COWBOYS: Barber 2-yard run (Folk kick). Thirteen plays, 74 yards in seven minutes.

4TH
SAINTS: Mike Bell 1-yard run (Hartley kick). Nine plays, 80 yards in 3:03.
SAINTS: Lance Moore 7-yard pass from Drew Brees (Hartley kick). Seven plays, 70 yards in 3:23.

TEAM STATISTICS

	SAINTS	COWBOYS
FIRST DOWNS	23	24
TOTAL OFFENSIVE PLAYS-YARDS (NET)	62-336	73-439
RUSHES-YARDS (NET)	13-65	36-145
PASSING YARDS (NET)	271	294
PASSES (COMP-ATT-INT)	29-45-1	22-34-0
PUNTS (NUMBER-AVG)	4-50.3	5-41.0
PUNT RETURNS-YARDS	2-4	2-35
KICKOFF RETURNS-YARDS	3-82	3-90
PENALTY YARDS	4-30	6-49
FUMBLES-LOST	2-2	0-0
TIME OF POSSESSION	23:34	36:26
FIELD GOALS (ATT-MADE)	1-1	2-1

Receiver Robert Meachem tries in vain to get past Dallas linebacker Bradie James, an ex-LSU standout, following a reception.

TED JACKSON/ THE TIMES-PICAYUNE

to keep winning, too, if they want to secure home-field advantage throughout the playoffs.

If they ended up tied after the regular season, the Vikings would win the tie-breaker based on conference record.

The Saints now were set to host the Tampa Bay Buccaneers (1-12) in eight days before finishing the regular season at Carolina (5-8) on Jan. 3.

"We talked a little bit about what's in front of us," New Orleans Coach Sean Payton said. "I think it's important that we continue to work and clean up some of the things we didn't do well. It will take a while to digest this loss, and it will sting a little bit going down. But it is what it is, and we'll get to work next week. We have two important games in front of us."

Payton rejected the notion the Saints' first loss might relieve some of the pressure of going for a perfect season or debating whether or not it was worth trying.

"No, it was disappointment. No type of relief," Payton said. "It's disappointment when you lose."

Once again, it seemed like destiny was trying to intervene on the Saints' behalf in the fourth quarter against the Cowboys.

After playing awful for three quarters and trailing 24-3 to start the fourth, New Orleans stepped up with a touchdown drive, a quick defensive stop and another touchdown drive.

Then, in a you-had-to-see-it-to-believe-it-moment,

Dallas' Nick Folk shanked a 24-yard field goal off the right upright with 2:16 remaining that would have given the Cowboys (9-5) a 10-point lead — an almost exact scenario that played out in the Saints' miracle comeback at Washington two weeks earlier in a 33-30 victory in overtime.

This time, however, the Saints fell short.

"When we walked out on that field, just down seven with 2:16 left, we felt like there was no doubt we were going to score and send it into OT," Brees said.

But Dallas' pass rush, which had stymied New Orleans for most of the game, continued to apply pressure — and the Saints used up 10 snaps and nearly two minutes just to move the ball to Dallas' 42-yard line.

The plan was to throw up a Hail Mary pass or two, but this time New Orleans' prayers went unanswered.

"As poorly as we played, we were fortunate just to have that chance with a final drive," Payton said. "But we couldn't get anything going really, and we didn't do a good enough job on those early plays (of the final drive). We left ourselves in a hole, basically, and we couldn't get out of it."

The Saints dug most of that hole during the first three quarters, when they played their worst 45 minutes of football all season and trailed 24-3.

The defense was porous, and the offense was just plain poor.

New Orleans safety Darren Sharper fails in his attempt to keep quarterback Tony Romo from gaining extra yards.

TED JACKSON / THE TIMES-PICAYUNE

COWBOYS | SAINTS
24 | 17

One dream comes to an end for New Orleans, but a bigger, Super one, still endures with the faithful of the Who Dat Nation

PETER FINNEY

What was there to say?

To me, it was a case of "America's Team" spoiling "America's Dream."

I said this thinking that there were enough newly converted Who Dats around the country caught up in the melancholy history of a star-crossed franchise riding a magic carpet to a perfect season.

That was the DREAM.

It was a dream terminated by a group of Dallas Cowboys dedicated to ending December miseries and playing their way into another postseason.

Now the more realistic dream remained for New Orleans, a "Super Bowl Dream," but it was filled with a big question.

Could a 13-0 Saints team that fell to 13-1 with their 24-17 setback to Dallas in front of their loving fans at the Superdome rediscover the magic that made them the darlings of the NFL?

After all seemed lost when the Cowboys took the second-half kickoff and drove to a 21-point lead, New Orleans dug down deep to make a game of it.

The Saints did that even after they returned the following kickoff 67 yards, and receiver Devery Henderson dropped a touchdown pass from quarterback Drew Brees in the end zone.

It was a dropped pass that loomed large as Brees brought the offense together for drives of 80 and 70 yards to start the fourth quarter.

Coach Sean Payton and New Orleans did not go gently into the night.

It was a matter of a defense, picked apart early, coming alive to apply more pressure to Dallas quarterback Tony Romo. It also was a matter of Brees, who was sacked four times, settling down in the face of pressure to keep his team in the hunt.

This was a game that largely belonged to two Cowboys.

It belonged to Romo, who was a monster in converting eight of 15 third-down opportunities (the Saints were 1-for-7).

And it belonged to linebacker DeMarcus Ware, who made the night a nightmare for Brees. Ware had two sacks and forced a fumble.

With the Saints thinking Hail Mary in the final seconds, it was Ware who pounced on Brees on the final play for the Saints, a fitting fingerprint for the Cowboys warrior.

As you watched the first quarter, it looked as if Dallas was playing with 14 players.

That was how dominant the white jerseys were, forcing Brees & Company to a couple of quick three-and-outs as they marched on touchdown drives of 79 and 60 yards.

When the score was 7-0, Dallas owned a 79-9 edge in yardage.

By the time the first quarter was history, the yardage margin had jumped to 195-35.

It was not a pretty sight.

New Orleans cornerback Malcolm Jenkins was spinning around as receiver Miles Austin ran by him to grab a 49-yard touchdown pass.

A 52-yard punt to Dallas' 12-yard line by Tomas Morstead was offset by allowing a 28-yard return.

A missed tackle by Saints safety Darren Sharper was a major contributor to a 26-yard completion.

After running back Reggie Bush brought the home crowd to life with a 29-yard burst off tackle, the Saints were missing a blitz pickup — and Brees was facing a third-and-20.

It was that kind of grim opening.

While the second quarter was pretty much a tossup as the Saints' defense began to apply more heat to Romo, New Orleans had to settle for a field goal after a first down at the Cowboys' 17. And, later, after moving from their 10 to Dallas' 44, the Saints watched an underthrown ball by Brees in the direction of Henderson result in an interception at the 4-yard line.

No, it was not a Who Dat night.

"Sometimes you've got to go through something like this to make you a better team," Brees said. "You learn from your mistakes, and you go on to your next game. Then the next one. Then the playoffs."

One dream was over.

Another endured.

BUCCANEERS | SAINTS
20   17

With a chance to defeat Tampa Bay, Garrett Hartley is left downtrodden following his failed 37-yard field goal attempt with nine seconds remaining in regulation.

RUSTY COSTANZA / THE TIMES-PICAYUNE

Said New Orleans'
Garrett Hartley
after missing a
37-yard field-goal
attempt for the
win: 'It's definitely
humbling.'

MICHAEL DeMOCKER /
THE TIMES-PICAYUNE

BUCCANEERS | SAINTS OT
20   17

BUC SHOT

The Saints are left with holes to fill after a shocking overtime setback to the Buccaneers, but all is not lost

By Nakia Hogan Staff writer

Some Who Dat fans now were holding off making reservations for Super Bowl XLIV on Feb. 7 in Miami.

The way the Saints were playing, it was no guarantee they would want to head to Sun Life Stadium for the big game.

This never was more obvious than New Orleans' 20-17 overtime loss to the Tampa Bay Buccaneers before 70,021 mostly stunned fans at the Superdome.

All was not lost, though.

Later that night, the Saints picked up home-field advantage in the NFC throughout the playoffs when host Carolina defeated the Minnesota Vikings 26-7.

But New Orleans was staggering into the postseason.

After rolling to a 17-0 lead, the Saints seemingly fell asleep at the wheel against the Buccaneers and allowed 20 consecutive points, including Connor Barth's 47-yard field goal with 8:06 remaining in overtime.

While the loss was the second in a row for New Orleans (13-2), it also marked its fourth consecutive sub-par performance.

In losing to the Buccaneers (3-12), the Saints were the first 13-win team in NFL history to lose to a previously two-win team.

"Things happen like that in the NFL, and we knew that coming in," New Orleans defensive end Will Smith said. "We knew that every team had a chance to beat us. Unfortunately, we've lost the last couple of games — but it's something that we have to rebound from. I definitely don't think it's the end of the world."

But it would end the Saints' record-breaking season early if they didn't find a way to cure their recent ills.

"I don't know if I'd call it the pressure mounting," said New Orleans quarterback Drew Brees, who completed 32 of 37 passes for 258 yards and a touchdown. "The fact is we need to play better."

The Saints had plenty of areas that needed attention after this setback:

▶ Offense — It went into the tank after scoring on its first three possessions, punting on four of its final six possessions and fumbling on another.

▶ Run defense — The Saints yielded 176 rushing yards to the Buccaneers, including 129 yards and a touchdown on 24 carries to Carnell "Cadillac" Williams.

▶ Third-down defense — For the second consecutive game, New Orleans failed to keep its opponent from routinely converting on third downs, allowing Tampa Bay to convert on seven of 12 attempts.

▶ Special teams — The Saints gave up a game-tying 77-yard punt return by Michael Spurlock with 2:25 remaining in regulation.

Still, New Orleans had a chance to win after blowing its largest lead in a loss since Sept. 17, 1989, when the Green Bay Packers overcame a 24-7 halftime deficit to beat the Saints 35-34 at Lambeau Field.

But with the score tied at 17 and nine seconds remaining against Tampa Bay, New Orleans kicker Garrett Hartley's 37-yard field-goal attempt sailed wide left, setting up overtime.

"He's played well for us," Saints Coach Sean Payton said of Hartley. "He's been battled-tested. I think it's a mistake if we just point to the missed kick, if we just point to the punt return, if we just point to one particular area. It's all our jobs to get it cleaned up.

"I've said this before. In our league, it's crisis or carnival because the stuff in the middle doesn't sell. Now you've hit some adversity."

Perhaps no Saints players hit the bottom as hard as Hartley.

Hartley, whose only miss in his two seasons with New Orleans was a 58-yard attempt in the Saints' 33-30 victory in overtime at Washington on Dec. 6, 2009, took responsibility for the loss.

"I felt great going out there," Hartley said. "(It was) just an opportunity to win another game. I kind of rushed myself a little bit. It was all me. The snap and hold were great. I just rushed myself.

"Knowing I let my teammates down is the worst thing. It's definitely humbling."

Time was running out for New Orleans to correct its recent deficiencies, however. With one regular-season game remaining at Carolina in seven days, the Saints had gone from a team with an unstoppable offense and an opportunistic defense to a squad that couldn't string

BUCS	1ST 0	2ND 3	3RD 0	4TH 14	OT 3	F 20
SAINTS	14	3	0	0	0	17

13-2

RECORD AFTER GAME 15

SCORING SUMMARY

1ST SAINTS: Pierre Thomas 8-yard run (Garrett Hartley kick). Nine plays, 75 yards in 4:29.
SAINTS: Robert Meachem 30-yard pass from Drew Brees (Hartley kick). Six plays, 51 yards in 2:59.

2ND SAINTS: Hartley 28-yard field goal. Ten plays, 83 yards in 5:07.
BUCCANEERS: Connor Barth 34-yard field goal. Eight plays, 52 yards in 1:45.

3RD NO SCORING

4TH BUCCANEERS: Carnell Williams 23-yard run Barth kick). Eight plays, 98 yards in 4:09.
BUCCANEERS: Micheal Spurlock 77-yard punt return (Barth kick).

OT BUCCANEERS: Barth 47-yard field goal. Eleven plays, 48 yards in 6:54.

INDIVIDUAL STATISTICS
RUSHING
SAINTS: Pierre Thomas 6-60, Lynell Hamilton 7-21.
BUCCANEERS: Carnell Williams 24-129, Derrick Ward 7-32.

DAVID GRUNFELD / THE TIMES-PICAYUNE
Connor Barth's 47-yard field goal with 8:06 remaining in overtime gives the Saints their second loss in a row.

PASSING
SAINTS: Drew Brees 32-37-258-1-0.
BUCCANEERS: Josh Freeman 21-31-271-0-2.

RECEIVING
SAINTS: Marques Colston 8-77, Reggie Bush 6-37.
BUCCANEERS: Antonio Bryant 5-52, Kellen Winslow 4-76.

INTERCEPTIONS
SAINTS: Tracy Porter 1, Darren Sharper 1.
BUCCANEERS: none.

SACKS
SAINTS: Charles Grant 1, Anthony Hargrove 1, Will Smith 1.
BUCCANEERS: Geno Hayes 1.

TACKLES (unassisted)
SAINTS: Malcolm Jenkins 8, Will Smith 7.
BUCCANEERS: Geno Hayes 9, Ronde Barber 8.

TEAM STATISTICS

	SAINTS	BUCS
FIRST DOWNS	23	24
TOTAL OFFENSIVE PLAYS-YARDS (NET)	61-373	68-439
RUSHES-YARDS (NET)	23-124	34-176
PASSING YARDS (NET)	249	263
PASSES (COMP-ATT-INT)	32-37-0	21-31-2
PUNTS (NUMBER-AVG)	4-40.3	3-39.0
PUNT RETURNS-YARDS	1-14	2-80
KICKOFF RETURNS-YARDS	3-65	5-116
PENALTY YARDS	2-14	7-42
FUMBLES-LOST	1-1	1-0
TIME OF POSSESSION	30:39	36:15
FIELD GOALS (ATT-MADE)	2-1	2-2

MICHAEL DeMOCKER / THE TIMES-PICAYUNE
New Orleans running back Pierre Thomas has a hard time focusing on the task at hand during the second quarter.

together four consecutive quarters of quality football.

For the second consecutive game, the Saints were left with a quiet and subdued locker room. They had to find that potion that had them feeling nearly invincible for the first 13 games — and their fans

thinking of a Super Bowl run.

"We have to get the swagger back that we had when we first started this," New Orleans defensive end Charles Grant said. "That swag is going to come back."

Saints quarterback Drew Brees and injured tight end Jeremy Shockey joined Coach Sean Payton on the sideline all game.

**MICHAEL DeMOCKER /
THE TIMES–PICAYUNE**

PANTHERS | SAINTS

23

10

113

With New Orleans starting quarterback Drew Bress taking a seat, Mark Brunell gets some playing time.

PANTHERS | SAINTS
23   10

HEALTHY CHOICE

Playoff-bound New Orleans holds out Drew Brees, decides to rest other starters in loss to Carolina

By Mike Triplett Staff writer

Sure, the Saints admitted that they were a little jealous of some of their NFC rivals.

While New Orleans was wrapping up its regular season with a lackluster 23-10 loss at Carolina, which essentially amounted to a fifth preseason game, fellow playoff teams such as the Minnesota Vikings, Green Bay Packers and Dallas Cowboys were having all the fun, routing their opponents by 37, 26 and 24 points.

But now that the postseason was officially under way, the Saints insisted they wouldn't trade places with any of those teams.

Despite their three-game losing streak, the Saints (13-3) were the No. 1 seed in the NFC. They still had a free pass into the second round of the playoffs, and they knew that any NFC team that wanted to reach Super Bowl XLIV on Feb. 7 in Miami had to come through New Orleans to get there.

"Listen, we'll be ready to play," said Saints Coach Sean Payton, who maintained that it was an easy decision for him to rest most of his starters — including quarterback Drew Brees — once New Orleans had clinched that No. 1 seed.

"I'm comfortable because it was the right thing to do," Payton said, explaining that there was "absolutely no data" to suggest whether it affected a team to enter the playoffs on a winning or losing streak.

"What's most important is your team, and knowing your team — and I like where we're at. I like this team a lot. I like the fact that we put ourselves in this position, and we'll be ready."

Most important, the Saints were expected to be healthy when they returned to the field during the post-season.

New Orleans exited its game in Charlotte, N.C., relatively unscathed, which was really the No. 1 priority. Kickoff returner Courtney Roby suffered an apparent concussion, and cornerback Malcolm Jenkins left early

SEAN PAYTON

Saints Coach Sean Payton draws praise for his plan of attack and the results that follow

By Mike Triplett Staff writer

Of all the benefits that came with a first-round bye in the playoffs, the one that might have served the Saints best was this: Coach Sean Payton had an extra week to tinker with his offense while getting ready for a matchup against the Arizona Cardinals on Jan. 16, 2010, at the Superdome.

"You give Payton the chalk and you give him two or three or four weeks extra time, look out," said Payton's friend and former boss, Jon Gruden, another of the game's highly regarded offensive minds who now analyzed the league on ESPN's "Monday Night Football." "I just have always been impressed by the way he puts together a game plan.

"It's never the same thing twice, and they've got more inventory in that offense than most teams in the league. Man, they have a lot of stuff, a lot of formations, personnel groupings — and a lot of talent. And a credit to Sean and (quarterback Drew Brees). They're like an extension of one another. It's like tag-team wrestling.

"While Drew is resting, Payton's scheming up something, then Drew goes out there and makes it happen. . . . He's got a quarterback who's like a terminator. He just has to program him."

When Gruden stopped by Saints training camp during the summer for a day, the two went up to Payton's office between practices and drew up plays.

It was hard to imagine that Payton slept, that he was not lying awake in bed every night running through every possible game scenario.

But Payton insisted that the 45-minute drive across the Causeway usually was enough time for him to switch his brain back into family mode. Usually.

"In the postseason, maybe that drive is coming at midnight or maybe you're spending that night here (at the practice facility)," Payton said. "But by the end of the week, you've got a pretty good idea of how you want to go

TED JACKSON / THE TIMES-PICAYUNE

PATRICK SEAN PAYTON   BORN December 29, 1963, in San Mateo, Calif.

REGULAR SEASON COACHING RESULTS	13-3 2009	8-8 2008	7-9 2007	13-3 2006

SEAN PAYTON

in and what your thoughts are.

"And it's a group effort. I lean heavily on (offensive coordinator) Pete Carmichael, (offensive line coach) Aaron Kromer and our offensive staff. I think a lot of times when the head coach happens to be the offensive play-caller, the work of the offensive staff gets overshadowed."

That process worked better than ever during the 2009 season.

Once again, the Saints led the NFL in yards gained and points scored. They were threatening the league record for points scored in a season until they hit the wall in the final three weeks.

Brees led the league with a passer rating of 109.6, the highest of his career, and he set the NFL record for completion percentage in a season (70.62 percent). The Saints also found more balance between the run and pass than they had in Payton's four-year tenure, ranking in the top six in the league in both categories.

Pro Football Hall of Fame quarterback Troy Aikman, who was able to appreciate the Saints up close in the Fox broadcast booth, also praised Payton.

"What I like is he calls plays without a great deal of fear," Aikman said. "I think there's a time when you have to be careful and all that, but for the most part he calls plays expecting his players to make plays. And obviously, the confidence he has in Drew Brees to run that offense has continued to grow — and they have a lot of weapons they can go to."

Payton said he and his staff were confident in the plan they had put together for the Cardinals.

"Looking back at my experience, when you look at the cut-ups at the end of the year of all the plays you've run offensively and defensively, often times the stuff that you ran in training camp are the ones you're most efficient at," Payton said. "So you begin to tinker with formations and dressing those things up, but you always have to be leery in games like this of trying to do too much."

"You give Payton the chalk and you give him two or three or four weeks extra time, look out. I just have always been impressed by the way he puts together a game plan."

JON GRUDEN
EX-NFL COACH,
TV ANALYST

ATTENDED Naperville Central High, Eastern Illinois University   NFL EXPERIENCE 12 years

SUPER SAINTS

SAINTS
45

CARDINALS
14

With the outcome no longer in doubt, New Orleans running back Reggie Bush takes it in all in from the sideline.

CHRIS GRANGER /
THE TIMES-PICAYUNE

Honorary captain
Deuce McAllister
leads the Saints out
of the tunnel and
onto the field before
the opening kickoff.

MICHAEL DeMOCKER /
THE TIMES-PICAYUNE

SAINTS | CARDINALS
45 14

REST ASSURED

Refreshed Saints prove a point and quash fears by routing the Cardinals in an NFC divisional playoff game

By Mike Triplett Staff writer

The Saints found the "on" switch.

After conserving their energy for the past month, the Saints flipped that switch and lit up the Superdome with a spectacular display of offense, defense, special teams, emotion and intensity.

New Orleans decimated the Arizona Cardinals with a 45-14 rout in an NFC divisional playoff game that validated everything the Saints had accomplished in the first 13 games of this season, the greatest in franchise history.

"So much for being rusty," New Orleans Coach Sean Payton said, practically gloating after his team showed absolutely no ill effects from a three-game losing streak that ended the regular season.

Said quarterback Drew Brees: "You can look at the 13-0 Saints or the ones that finished the season 0-3 — and we know that we're the 13-0 Saints. We played like that today."

Now they were one victory away from securing a spot in Super Bowl XLIV on Feb. 7 in Miami.

"It's going to be the biggest game in franchise history, no question about it," Saints linebacker Scott Fujita said, just minutes after the Saints had finished off their most impressive win in their 43 years. (Minnesota and 40-year old quarterback Brett Favre defeated the visiting Dallas Cowboys 34-3 the next day, setting up a Saints-Vikings matchup in the NFC championship game at the Superdome.)

Yes, New Orleans (14-3) was affected by the way it finished the regular season, playing lousy against visiting Dallas and visiting Tampa Bay, then resting their starters at Carolina in the regular-season finale and having to sit through a bye last weekend.

But the effect was a positive one.

Not only were the Saints healthy, but they were so fired up to play a meaningful game for the first time in three weeks that everybody on the field looked as if he was shot out of a cannon — from running back Reggie

SUPER SAINTS

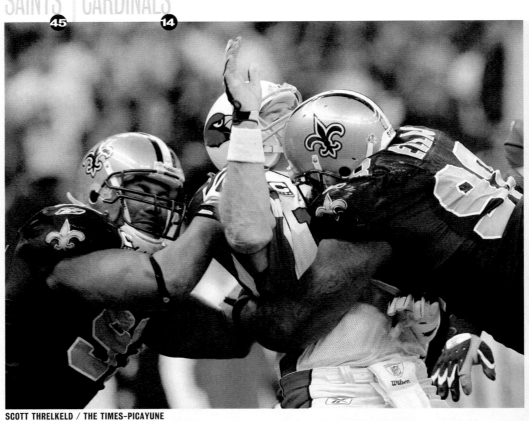

SCOTT THRELKELD / THE TIMES-PICAYUNE

Saints defensive end Will Smith, left, and defensive tackle Sedrick Ellis welcome quarterback Kurt Warner to the Superdome.

Bush, who was dynamic, to Brees, who fired off three touchdown passes, to an attacking defense that swarmed Arizona quarterback Kurt Warner.

"Hey, we were tired of hearing (the questions about rust), and we were chomping at the bit and just wanting to get it going," Brees said. "This is why we fought so hard in the season. This is why we worked so hard in the offseason, just to give yourself an opportunity to be in the playoffs, to succeed in the playoffs — and in the end win a championship. That's been our main focus the entire time."

Payton gambled by resting his starters against the Panthers, but he said a talk with mentor Bill Parcells a couple of weeks earlier helped reinforce the confidence he had in his choice and his team.

"He said, 'You know your team better than anyone,'" Payton said. "That bye week for us was critical, getting guys healthy and

rested for this game."

Against the Cardinals (11-7), the Saints trailed 7-0 one play into the game. Tailback Tim Hightower broke free for a 70-yard touchdown run against a porous Saints' defense that had struggled badly down the stretch.

New Orleans didn't panic.

"We knew it wasn't going to be a 7-0 game," Saints safety Darren Sharper said.

New Orleans responded with a 10-play, 72-yard touchdown drive that ended with Lynell Hamilton's 1-yard touchdown run.

On Arizona's next play, the Saints' defense struck back.

Cornerback Randall Gay forced a fumble at the end of receiver Jerheme Urban's 28-yard catch, and Sharper recovered.

Four plays later, Brees hit tight end Jeremy Shockey with a 17-yard touchdown pass.

"Hey, our mentality is we're going to try to score every time we touch the ball. There's a confidence level there that is unique, but

The Saints' Reggie Bush turns on the afterburners during his 46-yard touchdown scamper in the first quarter.
SCOTT THRELKELD / THE TIMES-PICAYUNE

SUPER SAINTS

	1ST	2ND	3RD	4TH	F
CARDS	7	7	0	0	14
SAINTS	21	14	10	0	45

TED JACKSON / THE TIMES PICAYUNE

INDIVIDUAL STATISTICS

RUSHING
SAINTS: Reggie Bush 5-84, Pierre Thomas 13-52.
CARDINALS : Tim Hightower 6-87, Chris Wells 5-7.

PASSING
SAINTS: Drew Brees 23-32-247-3-0.
CARDINALS: Kurt Warner 17-26-205-0-1, Matt Leinart 7-10-61-0-0.

RECEIVING
SAINTS: Marques Colston 6-83, Devery Henderson 4-80.
CARDINALS: Early Doucet 8-68, Larry Fitzgerald 6-77.

INTERCEPTIONS
SAINTS: Will Smith 1.
CARDINALS: none.

SACKS
SAINTS: Sedrick Ellis 1.
CARDINALS: none.

TACKLES (unassisted)
SAINTS: Randall Gay 7, Scott Shanle 6.
CARDINALS: Karlos Dansby 8, Adrian Wilson 8.

GAME STATISTICS
Attendance: 70,149 at Superdome

SCORING SUMMARY

1ST
CARDINALS: Tim Hightower 70-yard run (Neil Rackers kick). One play, 70 yards in 19 seconds.
SAINTS: Lynell Hamilton 1-yard run (Garrett Hartley kick). Ten plays, 72 yards in 5:24.
SAINTS: Jeremy Shockey 17-yard pass from Drew Brees (Hartley kick). Four plays, 37 yards in 1:58.
SAINTS: Reggie Bush 46-yard run (Hartley kick). Five plays, 77 yards in 2:54.

2ND
CARDINALS: Chris Wells 4-yard run (Rackers kick). Nine plays, 80 yards in 5:07.
SAINTS: Devery Henderson 44-yard pass from Brees (Hartley kick). Six plays, 83 yards in 2:52.
SAINTS: Marques Colston 2-yard pass from Brees (Hartley kick). Eight plays, 27 yards in 4:38.

3RD
SAINTS: Hartley 43-yard field goal. Six plays, 39 yards in 2:10.
SAINTS: Bush 83-yard punt return (Hartley kick).

4TH NO SCORING

TEAM STATISTICS

	SAINTS	CARDINALS
FIRST DOWNS	27	15
TOTAL OFFENSIVE PLAYS-YARDS (NET)	66-418	52-359
RUSHES-YARDS (NET)	34-171	15-101
PASSING YARDS (NET)	247	258
PASSES (COMP-ATT-INT)	23-32-0	24-36-1
PUNTS (NUMBER-AVG)	4-42.8	6-43.5
PUNT RETURNS-YARDS	3-109	0-0
KICKOFF RETURNS-YARDS	2-37	5-139
PENALTY YARDS	6-44	3-22
FUMBLES-LOST	0-0	3-1
TIME OF POSSESSION	36:27	23:33
FIELD GOALS (ATT-MADE)	1-1	1-0

SUPER SAINTS

that's the way we play," said Brees, who completed 23 of 32 passes for 247 yards and three touchdowns. "After they got that first touchdown, all we're thinking is, 'Respond.'

"We went down and got that score to kind of calm the jitters a little bit, then we got that turnover and went down and scored again — and it was off to the races from there."

That was an understatement.

After the Saints forced a quick punt by Arizona, New Orleans responded again with a sensational 46-yard touchdown run by Bush, who bounced off a potential tackler, sidestepped another and shot the final 40 yards like he was back at Southern California where he picked up a Heisman Trophy.

In the second quarter, the Saints added a 44-yard touchdown pass from Brees to receiver Devery Henderson on a flea-flicker, and a 2-yard touchdown pass to receiver Marques Colston. In the third quarter, they added a 43-yard field goal by Garrett Hartley, and the exclamation point — an 83-yard touchdown on a punt return by Bush, his first of the season.

"That was vintage Reggie Bush," Sharper said.

And that was no accident.

Payton had a specific plan for keeping Bush fresh over the course of the season, limiting his use to prevent too much wear and tear on his surgically repaired left knee.

More than anyone on the field, it looked like Bush couldn't wait to break out of the starting gate once the playoffs arrived.

He sprinted past honorary captain Deuce McAllister after the team was introduced, holding a baseball bat with the inscription "Bring the Wood" that Payton handed out to all the players the day before. Then he stayed out on the field, bat in hand, firing up the kickoff coverage team before the opening kickoff.

"These types of games are the games you live for. As a competitor, as an athlete, this is what you work for through the offseason, training camp, the preseason," said Bush, who showed as much toughness as he did speed against the Cardinals, fighting for first downs on short gains and lowering his shoulder into defenders. He finished with 84 yards on five carries and 24 yards on four receptions, plus 109 yards on three punt returns.

The Saints' defense brought the wood, too.

After feeling dissed by everyone who predicted a repeat of last week's 51-45 overtime victory by the Cardinals over the Green Bay Packers in a wild-card game in Glendale, Ariz., Saints defenders were eager to remind everyone that they were a worthwhile unit during the team's 13-0 start.

Defensive end Will Smith made an outstanding, ath-

MICHAEL DeMOCKER / THE TIMES-PICAYUNE

Cardinals receiver Jerheme Urban looses the ball, with cornerback Randall Gay (20) and safety Roman Harper eyeing the situation.

letic play when he batted a Warner pass to himself and intercepted it in the second quarter, setting up the Colston touchdown. End Bobby McCray laid a hellacious hit on Warner during Smith's return that knocked Warner out of the game for the remainder of the half.

Defensive tackle Sedrick Ellis repeatedly was disruptive up the middle, and linebackers Fujita and Scott Shanle were constantly hounding the ball.

Meanwhile, New Orleans cornerbacks Jabari Greer and Tracy Porter kept Pro Bowl receiver Larry Fitzgerald quiet for most of the game. Fitzgerald's first catch came on the final drive of the first half.

"I don't know who was predicting all those 37-35 scores and all those points," Sharper said. "You forget sometimes how good your defense is when you lose . . . but we knew we'd come out to play. With all our guys back, we're a different team."

The Saints didn't need to do a lot of blitzing to disrupt Warner, who was practically perfect against the Packers. He completed 17 of 26 passes for 205 yards with an interception against the Saints.

After Hightower's initial run, the Cardinals were held to 31 rushing yards.

"I just think all the way around we were ready to play this game, and that showed," Brees said.

TED JACKSON / THE TIMES PICAYUNE

DARREN MALLORY SHARPER BORN November 3, 1975, in Richmond, Va. HEIGHT 6 feet 2 WEIGHT 210 lbs.

14	**14**	**71**	**0.5**	**9**	**3**
GAMES	STARTS	TACKLES	SACKS	INTERCEPTIONS	TOUCHDOWNS

ATTENDED **Hermitage High School, College of William & Mary** NFL EXPERIENCE: **13 seasons**

DARREN SHARPER

Saints safety Darren Sharper gets his wish: The Saints to battle his former team — the Vikings — in the NFC championship game

By Mike Triplett Staff writer

The Saints knew it was only going to get tougher in the playoffs.

That point was truly driven home, though, when they watched the way their next opponent, the Minnesota Vikings, dominate the Dallas Cowboys in a 34-3 rout in an NFC divisional playoff game Jan. 17, 2010, in Minneapolis.

Once again, the Saints (14-3) and Vikings (13-4) had emerged as the two best teams in the NFC, and one of them would end a serious drought.

The Vikings hadn't advanced to a Super Bowl in 33 years, and the Saints were one of five teams never to reach a Super Bowl (the other four were the Browns, Lions, Jaguars and Oilers).

New Orleans safety Darren Sharper made no secret that this was the matchup he wanted — a revenge game against his former team with a berth in Super Bowl XLIV on Feb. 7 in Miami on the line.

Minnesota had let him get away in free agency after he spent the previous four years in Minnesota.

"You know who I want; you know who I want," Sharper said after the Saints had defeated the Arizona Cardinals 45-14 in a divisional playoff game at the Superdome the day before the Vikings-Cowboys game. "It would add a little bit to it, a little more excitement. You know, I'll be familiar with a lot of faces across the football field."

Following the Vikings' victory, Sharper now would face quarterback Brett Favre, a longtime former teammate and former rival. They played together for eight years with the Green Bay Packers before Sharper moved on to the Vikings.

And now they were both trying to return to the Super Bowl for the first time in 12 years.

"It's funny how it can transpire that we have a chance to meet each other to go to the Super Bowl," said Sharper, who had nine interceptions — three returned for touchdowns — in the regular season. "I had a chance to talk to him when he was thinking about going to Minnesota, and I told him, 'Listen, if you go there, you guys have a Super Bowl-caliber team. You've got all the pieces in place.'"

Advancing to Super Bowl XLIV weighed heavily on everyone's mind.

"None of these games are going to be easy," said New Orleans tailback Pierre Thomas. "You're that close to the Big Show."

If the Saints need any reminder of just how special and elusive that "Big Show" was, they turned to Sharper.

He made his one and only Super Bowl appearance as a rookie in Green Bay, and this was the first time he had made it back to the NFC championship game since.

"Being a naive rookie and playing in the Super Bowl my rookie year and having Brett Favre, them (having won the Super Bowl) the year before, you're thinking, 'Oh man, this is gonna be easy,'" Sharper recalled. "So I was thinking I'd have plenty of chances to get back there. Hopefully, I can get back there."

SAINTS | VIKINGS OT

31

28

NEW ORLEANS SAINTS
NFC CHAMPIONS

Teammates surround Garrett Hartley after he kicked a 40-yard field goal in overtime to propel the Saints to their first Super Bowl.
TED JACKSON / THE TIMES-PICAYUNE

SUPER SAIN

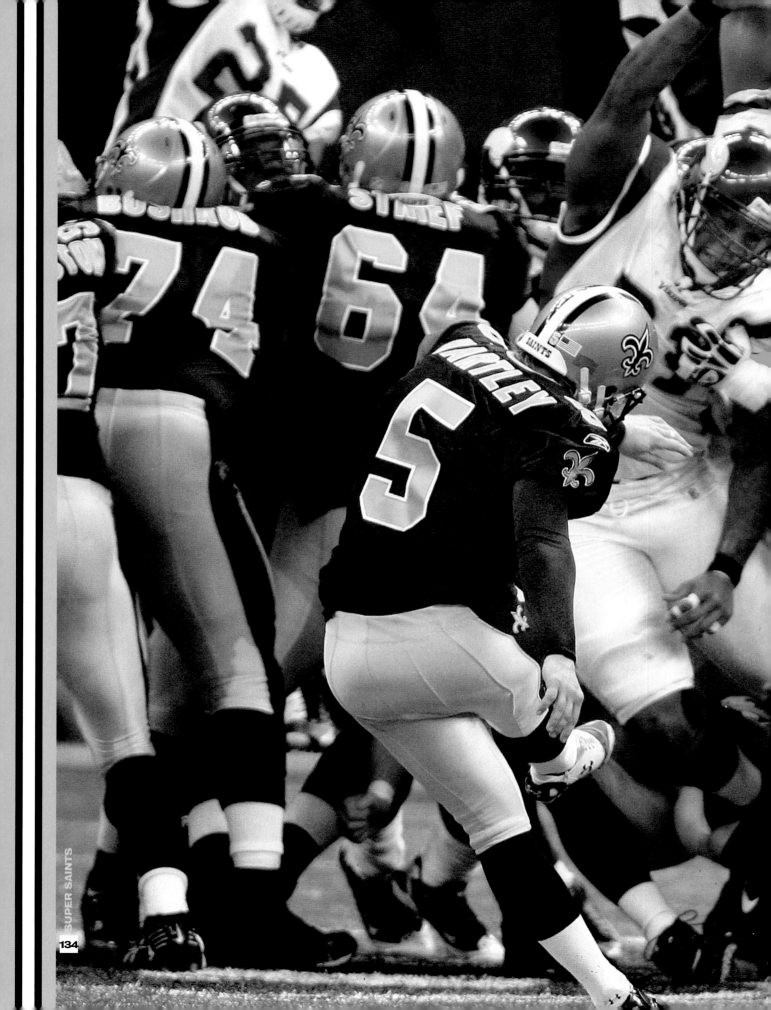

With a spot in Super Bowl XLIV on the line, New Orleans' Garrett Hartley connects on a 40-yard field goal in overtime.

ELIOT KAMENITZ /
THE TIMES-PICAYUNE

SAINTS | VIKINGS OT
31 | 28

ALIVE & KICKING

Garrett Hartley's field goal in overtime lifts New Orleans past Minnesota and into Super Bowl XLIV

By Nakia Hogan Staff writer

There were 42 years worth of demons, 42 years of mostly struggles, 42 years of waiting until next year.

Not anymore. This, the 43rd season of the Saints, was different.

In one swing of Garrett Hartley's right leg, the Saints kicked away their demons, booted out their past struggles and ended the wait.

The Saints were going to Super Bowl XLIV.

Hartley's 40-yard field goal in overtime of the Saints' thrilling 31-28 victory over the Minnesota Vikings in the NFC championship game guaranteed them a spot.

"I just knew when it came off my foot it was going to split the bars," said Hartley, a second-year pro. "I just turned around and put my hands up in the air and hugged (holder Mark) Brunnell. This team is headed to Miami."

It also sent jubilant Saints players rushing to mob Hartley, made Black & Gold confetti rain down from the rafters and sent a crowd of 71,276, the largest to watch the team play at the Superdome, into a frenzy.

It brought Louisiana Gov. Bobby Jindal down to the field to congratulate the team, moved the Saints' 82-year-old owner, Tom Benson, to bogeying around the turf with his umbrella, and brought grown men to tears.

Through all the Mardi Gras parades, Sugar Bowls, Jazz and Essence festivals, New Orleans had never partied like that.

More than four years after Hurricane Katrina wrecked this city, severely damaged the Superdome and left unprecedented damages, some questioned if New Orleans would recover, let alone party like there was no tomorrow.

"This is for everybody in this city," Coach Sean Payton said. "This stadium used to have holes in it and used to be wet. It's not wet anymore. This is for the city of New Orleans."

Afterward, Benson's message to his team was short

SUPER SAINTS

135

SCOTT THRELKELD / THE TIMES-PICAYUNE

The Saints didn't sack the Vikings' Brett Favre, but they repeatedly were able to make their presence felt on the 40 year old.

and to the point: "Thank you."

It had taken 43 years to get to that point, rising from an expansion team whose first roster was pieced together by rejects from other teams.

The franchise, which began in 1967, had not appeared in a playoff game until 1987 and had no playoff win until 2000, and was formerly known as the Aints. Its fans once donned bags on their heads while watching from the stands, but against the Vikings the Saints made the last four-plus decades irrelevant by accepting the George S. Halas Memorial Trophy.

"I actually had to just take a seat and really just enjoy it all and let it sink in, especially with the fans," said New Orleans linebacker Jonathan Vilma, who intercepted a pass thrown by quarterback Brett Favre and recovered a fumble. "The fans really were more excited than us after the game."

Next up for the Saints: the Indianapolis Colts, who defeated the visiting New York Jets 30-17 in the AFC championship game earlier that day, on Feb. 7 at Sun Life Stadium.

"It's a moment that I've been waiting for a long time for," New Orleans quarterback Drew Brees said.

The moment nearly didn't happen, though.

While the Saints' defense forced five turnovers and routinely hit Minnesota quarterback Brett Favre, 40, hard, New Orleans never gained much separation from the Vikings.

Brees, a prolific passer who typically had his way against opposing defenses, didn't get the offense rolling the way it had for much of the season.

Brees completed 17 of 31 passes for 197 yards and three touchdowns. He did not throw an interception, but the offense sputtered for much of the second half — and

TED JACKSON / THE TIMES-PICAYUNE

Late in regulation and with Minnesota in field-goal range, cornerback Tracy Porter is on the move after intercepting a pass by quarterback Brett Favre.

New Orleans was just three of 12 on third down.

"It wasn't pretty," Saints running back Reggie Bush said. "It was ugly as matter of fact, but we got the win. I've never seen a field goal look so pretty in my entire life."

The only reason New Orleans had an opportunity at a field goal in overtime was because the defense came up with a critical stop.

With the Vikings on their way to a potential winning field-goal attempt in the closing seconds of regulation, facing a third-and-15 from the Saints' 38-yard line, Favre was flushed from the pocket and attempted to throw the ball back across the field.

Cornerback Tracy Porter intercepted the pass intended for Sidney Rice at the 22, and he returned the ball to the Saints' 48 with seven seconds remaining.

Favre, who completed 28 of 46 passes for 310 yards,

with a touchdown and two interceptions, didn't get another chance.

"We've had no three turnover games this year, so to have five against a very good football team is very difficult to overcome," Minnesota Coach Brad Childress said.

In overtime, the Saints won the coin toss and made their run, or better yet, kick at history.

After Pierre Thomas returned the kickoff 40 yards to the Saints' 39, New Orleans took 10 plays — including a pivotal 2-yard leap by Thomas on fourth-and-1 and two Minnesota penalties — to set up Hartley's winning kick.

Hartley, who admitted to battling a serious case of nerves the night before as he prepared for the game, was faced with his first game-winning attempt since missing from a similar spot against the visiting Tampa Bay Buccaneers on Dec. 27, 2009, at the Superdome.

He missed the 37-yard attempt for the win that day,

GAME STATISTICS
Attendance: 71,276 at Superdome

SCORING SUMMARY

1ST
VIKINGS: Adrian Peterson 19-yard run (Ryan Longwell kick). Ten plays, 80 yards in 5:25.
SAINTS: Pierre Thomas 38-yard pass from Drew Brees. (Garrett Hartley kick). Seven plays, 76 yards in 3:05.
VIKINGS: Sidney Rice 5-yard pass from Brett Favre (Longwell kick). Ten plays, 73 yards in 4:19.

2ND
SAINTS: Devery Henderson 9-yard pass from Brees (Hartley kick). Seven plays, 64 yards in 2:51.

3RD
SAINTS: Pierre Thomas 9-yard run (Hartley kick). Four plays, 37 yards in 2:04.
VIKINGS: Peterson 1-yard run (Longwell kick). Nine plays, 80 yards in 5:21.

4TH
SAINTS: Reggie Bush 5-yard pass from Brees (Hartley kick). Three plays, 7 yards in 1:31.
VIKINGS: Peterson 2-yard run. (Longwell kick). Seven plays, 57 yards in 2:59.

OT
SAINTS: Hartley 40-yard field goal. Ten plays, 39 yards in 4:45.

TEAM STATISTICS

	SAINTS	VIKINGS
FIRST DOWNS	15	31
TOTAL OFFENSIVE PLAYS-YARDS (NET)	55-257	82-475
RUSHES-YARDS (NET)	23-68	36-165
PASSING YARDS (NET)	189	310
PASSES (COMP-ATT-INT)	17-31-0	28-46-2
PUNTS (NUMBER-AVG)	7-51.3	4-39
PUNT RETURNS-YARDS	1-0	3-15
KICKOFF RETURNS-YARDS	6-183	2-33
PENALTY YARDS	9-88	5-32
FUMBLES-LOST	3-1	6-3
TIME OF POSSESSION	27:56	36:49
FIELD GOALS (ATT-MADE)	1-1	0-0

SCOTT THRELKELD / THE TIMES PICAYUNE

INDIVIDUAL STATISTICS

RUSHING
SAINTS: Pierre Thomas 14-61, Reggie Bush 7-8.
VIKINGS: Adrian Peterson 25-122, Chester Taylor 6-28.

PASSING
SAINTS: Drew Brees 17-31-197-3-0.
VIKINGS: Brett Favre 28-46-310-1-2.

RECEIVING
SAINTS: Devery Henderson 4-39, David Thomas 3-32.
VIKINGS: Bernard Berrian 9-102, Percy Harvin 5-38.

INTERCEPTIONS
SAINTS: Tracy Porter 1, Jonathan Vilma 1.
VIKINGS: none.

SACKS
SAINTS: none.
VIKINGS: Ray Edwards 1.

TACKLES (unassisted)
SAINTS: Scott Shanle 8, Tracy Porter 8.
VIKINGS: Chad Greenway 7, Madieu Williams 5.

MICHAEL DeMOCKER / THE TIMES-PICAYUNE
With the outcome hanging in the balance, the Saints' Pierre Thomas holds onto the ball while gaining 2 yards on fourth-and-1 in overtime.

but against Minnesota he was in no mood to miss another. His field goal sailed down the middle to set off a wild celebration.

"Last night, I really couldn't sleep too well," Hartley said. "I called my dad (Bill) at 2:15 in the morning, and I said 'Dad, I have a feeling I'm going to hit a game-winner from 42 yards on the right hash.' I think I was off by about 2 yards."

The Saints overcame a nearly disastrous miscue late in the first half and managed to play the Vikings to a tie at 14 heading into halftime. Two plays after Bush muffed a punt at the Saints' 10 that the Vikings' Kenny Onatolu recovered with 1:13 remaining in the first half, Favre and running back Adrian Peterson, who lost two fumbles, failed to execute a handoff — and linebacker Scott Fujita pounced on the ball.

The Saints took a 21-14 lead in the third quarter on Thomas' 9-yard touchdown run.

But Minnesota running back Adrian Peterson, who had 25 carries for 122 yards and three touchdowns, tied the score at 21 on a 1-yard touchdown run.

Brees' 5-yard touchdown pass to Bush gave New Orleans a 28-21 lead before Peterson closed out the scoring in regulation with a 2-yard touchdown run.

But there was no stopping the Saints, who had added motivation from Payton, who handed out purple baseball bats to his team, reminding his players to "bring the wood," and Pro Football Hall of Fame safety Ronnie Lott, who gave a pregame speech.

"This is a pretty surreal moment," Brees said. "Words just can't describe the feeling. When you think back to four years ago, coming back here post-Katrina, Sean Payton's first year, I remember the phone call that he gave me, telling me that he wants me to be their quarterback.

"I could never have imagined that things would have worked out the way that they have, but we had a goal and we had a dream back then — and it was to have this opportunity to go and play for a Super Bowl championship"

139

As the Saints take care of business against the Vikings, memories of a franchise's ups and downs quickly flow

PETER FINNEY

They believed.

The Saints, a franchise that lost more games than you can count to field-goal attempts that went wide right or wide left, beat the Minnesota Vikings 31-28 in overtime in the NFC championship game at the Superdome, winning its biggest game with a perfect 40-yard field goal that traveled from Poydras Street toward Girod Street.

The Saints did it, securing a spot against quarterback Peyton Manning and the Indianapolis Colts in Super Bowl XLIV on Feb. 7 in Miami.

Garrett Hartley, 23, celebrated with holder Mark Brunell after kicking the winning field goal against the Vikings. Hartley, whose right foot put the Who Dats into a frenzy, was not around for the jeers and tears surrounding the onetime Keystone Kops of the NFL, the Gang That Couldn't Shoot Straight.

Here was a franchise born on All-Saints Day in 1966, that took 21 years to celebrate its first winning season, 35 years to win its first playoff game and 42 years to play for a world championship.

Suddenly, there was a confetti shower inside the Superdome and you probably reminisced of those melancholy Sundays gone bye.

You had to think of Al Hirt and his trumpet, trying to ease the sorrow at Tulane Stadium.

You had to think of the pigeons, and the fireworks at those halftime shows, and you had to think of a winning 63-yard field goal by Tom Dempsey.

You had to think of those miserable long-ago losses to the Atlanta Falcons, thanks to those game-ending Big Ben plays.

Finally, all the comedy, all the catcalls, all the misery during the reign of the bag-heads, had given way to Kismet.

Somewhere, up there, Buddy Diliberto was smiling.

Here we had Hero Hartley telling us he dreamed the night before the NFC championship game of making a game-winning kick.

We had New Orleans Coach Sean Payton telling us his advice to his kicker before the big kick was simple: "Just aim for the fleur-de-lis sign behind the uprights."

Fortunately, all Vikings quarterback Brett Favre was able to do was just stand there and watch.

Favre had passed for a touchdown against the Saints, and he had set up three other scores in one more amazing display by a 40-year-old triggerman.

It took an outstanding effort by the Saints' defense to keep Favre from throwing for more than 310 yards, to intercept him twice, to force a season-high six fumbles and recover three. What helped make Favre effective were three touchdowns and 122 rushing yards by Adrian Peterson.

Meanwhile, New Orleans quarterback Drew Brees, under mounting pressure as the game went on, found time to throw for three touchdowns — then engineered a crucial field-goal drive in overtime.

It was a drive given life by Saints running back Pierre Thomas, who was playing with three broken ribs.

Thomas got it going with a 40-yard kickoff return in overtime, and later — with the Saints' facing fourth-and-1 at the Vikings' 43, went airborne for 2 yards that kept the chains moving.

The fireworks began with a rousing first half that saw the Vikings march 80 yards, a stretch during which Favre displayed his mettle by doing an excellent job in shutting out the Saints' 12th man.

With the crowd at fever pitch, No. 4 went about his business by mixing several short completions with rushes of 8, 11 and 6 yards before Peterson galloped the final 19 yards as he ran through the arms of safety Darren Sharper.

New Orleans' response was immediate, not to mention familiar, with Brees going to the air three times for modest yardage, before connecting with running back Thomas in the right flat — then watched Thomas turn medium yardage into a 38-yard touchdown with a sharp cutback.

Whereupon, it was Favre's turn to see what he could do — and he responded by taking the Vikings 73 yards, ending the drive by firing a 5-yard bullet into the hands of receiver Sidney Rice on third-and-goal.

Brees was not finished.

At the start of the second quarter, facing a third-and-10 at the Saints' 36, Brees connected with running back Reggie Bush for 28 yards. Three plays later and New Orleans trailing 14-7, he was breaking out of the pocket to connect with Devery Henderson for a 9-yard touchdown.

In the closing minute of the first half after Bush

Quarterback Drew Brees holds for all to see the George S. Halas Memorial Trophy after the Saints won the NFC championship.

ELIOT KAMENTIZ / THE TIMES-PICAYUNE

muffed a punt to give Minnesota the ball at the Saints' 10, Favre let Bush off the hook when he and Peterson failed to make a connection on a handoff. The ball came loose, and linebacker Scott Fujita recovered the fumble.

The teams matched touchdowns in the third and fourth quarters, with the Vikings twice rubbing out seven-point leads.

It was that kind of war down to the end.

At least one New Orleans-based Who Dat already had made his plans for Super Bowl XLIV, which was scheduled for nine days before Mardi Gras.

He said: "Breakfast will be at the French Market. A two-block walk for Bloody Marys at Margaritaville. Catch a Mardi Gras parade on Canal Street. A shrimp po-boy at Johnny's in the Quarter. A Hurricane at Pat O'Brien's. Stroll over to the Superdome parking lot for tailgating. Early dinner at Galatoire's. More Hurricanes at Pat O'Brien's. Watch the Saints beat the Colts at the Absinthe House. Back to Canal Street for another parade. Close out the night on Bourbon Street. Sleep till Tuesday. Get ready for the draft. Geaux Super Bowl champions."

'WHO DAT' IS FOR THE PEOPLE, NOT THE NFL

By Ed Anderson
Staff writer

Louisiana State Attorney General Buddy Caldwell didn't see the need to file a lawsuit against the NFL over who owned "Who Dat" or the fleur-de-lis.

Caldwell said he and members of his staff spent an hour on Feb. 1, 2010, with lawyers for the NFL over trademark claims to the slogan and symbol that had become attached to the Saints.

Caldwell said the bottom line was that the NFL "is conceding it has no exclusive rights to the fleur-de-lis and no exclusive rights to 'Who Dat' and offshoots of 'Who Dat,' and no exclusive rights to the colors black and gold."

Confirming what the NFL said in clarifying statements released three days earlier, Caldwell said merchants could sell products with the Who Dat phrase and the fleur-de-lis as long as they didn't claim the items were officially licensed NFL items.

ELIOT KAMENITZ / THE TIMES-PICAYUNE

DON'T WORRY BUDDY D, SAINTS FANS HAVE YOU COVERED

Buddy Diliberto (inset) vowed to wear a dress if the Saints made the Super Bowl. Unfortunately, the legendary sportscaster, who died Jan. 7, 2005, wasn't around to enjoy in the celebration of the Saints reaching Super Bowl XLIV in Miami. On Jan. 31, 2010 — seven days before the Saints squared off against the Colts in the NFL championship game at Sun Life Stadium, fans in the Crescent City paid off Buddy D's debt on a day filled with tears and laughter.

TOUCHDOWN

Sun Life Stadium in Miami was the site of Super Bowl XLIV.

CHRIS GRANGER / THE TIMES-PICAYUNE

THE SAINTS ARRIVE FOR SUPER BOWL XLIV IN MIAMI, WITH A MATCHUP AGAINST THE COLTS LOOMING

TED JACKSON / THE TIMES-PICAYUNE

In advance of Super Bowl XLIV, the Saints' team and staff flew into Miami International Airport on Feb. 1, 2010, and prominently displayed is a fleur-de-lis. The Who Dat Nation soon followed.

SAINTS | COLTS

31 17

With the Saints leading 24-17, cornerback Tracy Porter's 74-yard interception return for a touchdown with 3:12 remaining seals the Colts' fate.

SCOTT THRELKELD / THE TIMES-PICAYUNE

SAINTS | COLTS
31 **17**

WORLD CHAMPIONS!

The Saints put an exclamation point on a magical season by overtaking the Colts in Super fashion

By Mike Triplett Staff writer

After the confetti had dropped, after the tears were shed, after they stood in front of the cameras and the microphones and tried to put the greatest performances of their professional lives in perspective, Saints Coach Sean Payton and quarterback Drew Brees shared a quiet moment together.

They hopped on the back of a golf cart, each with a hand on the shiny silver Vince Lombardi Trophy that rested in Payton's lap, each with a wide grin stuck across their faces.

"Don't you just want it to slow down and last longer?" Payton said to Brees.

Lucky for them, the feeling wasn't going away any time soon, now that the Saints were NFL champions for the first time in their 43-year history, thanks to a thrilling 31-17 victory over the Indianapolis Colts in Super Bowl XLIV at Sun Life Stadium.

Who believed Dat?

"New Orleans is back, and we showed the whole world!" owner Tom Benson exclaimed on the stage at midfield, as the thousands of Who Dats in attendance screamed their approval.

Payton followed him, saying there wasn't enough room on the stage for all the players who made it happen, and then he turned the microphone over to Brees, introducing him as "the MVP of this Super Bowl and the MVP of our league."

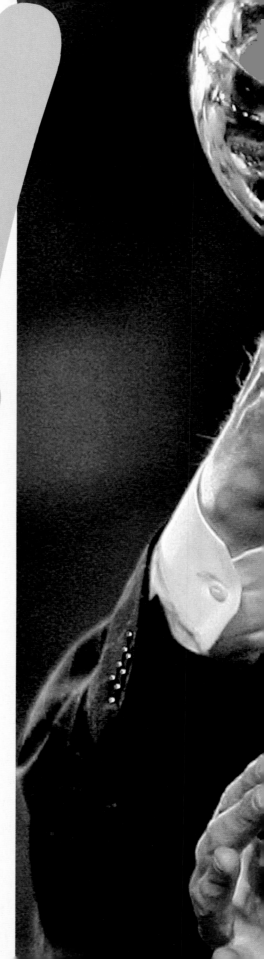

Coach Sean Payton has a firm grip on the Vince Lombardi Trophy after New Orleans vanquished Indianapolis.

The setting for Super Bowl XLIV at Sun Life Stadium is awe inspiring, and the play between the Saints and Colts lived up to the hype.

CHRIS GRANGER / THE TIMES-PICAYUNE

It was hard to argue after Brees' brilliant performance on the game's brightest stage.

To earn that trophy, New Orleans had to navigate its way through three potential Pro Football Hall of Fame quarterbacks in the Arizona Cardinals' Kurt Warner, the Minnesota Vikings' Brett Favre and Indianapolis' Peyton Manning.

Brees was better than all of them, especially in the NFL title game when he directed the go-ahead touchdown drive and two-point conversion midway through the fourth quarter.

"It's unbelievable. I mean it's sunk in, but I don't know if it's really sunk in yet," said Brees, who said he didn't usually have trouble sleeping but admitted that he hardly slept the previous two nights as he ran through all the possible scenarios he might face against Indianapolis.

When it happened for real, the Saints took possession of the ball at their 41-yard line with 10:39 remaining, trailing 17-16.

After a 12-yard run by Reggie Bush, Brees took over.

Brees completed all eight of his passes over the next nine plays to eight receivers, including a 2-yard touchdown strike to tight end Jeremy Shockey and a two-point conversion pass to receiver Lance Moore, giving the Saints a 24-17 lead with 5:42 remaining.

"Listen, we spread the ball around all year long. You never knew when it was gonna be time for someone else to step up," said Brees, who completed 32 of 39 passes for 288 yards, with two touchdown passes and no interceptions. "And I can't say enough about our offensive line,

going up against one of the best pass-rushing defenses in the league."

Manning, who was the league's regular-season MVP, didn't match Brees' heroics.

Late in the fourth quarter, Manning — a New Orleans native — threw an interception right into the arms of cornerback Tracy Porter, who returned it 74 yards for the game-clinching score.

"It was great film study. The coaching staff did a great job of preparing us for that route," said Porter, who explained that once he saw receiver Austin Collie go in motion, he knew what route his man — receiver Reggie Wayne — would run, and he jumped in front of it.

"He made a great play. Made a great play. That's all I can say about it. Porter made a heck of a play," Manning said. "They deserved the win today."

The Saints' victory was amazing because it took a total team effort, which was a microcosm of their entire season.

After the Colts jumped to a 10-0 lead, the Saints' offense and defense settled down.

Brees said they talked before the game about needing to just "weather the storm" and make sure their nerves and adrenaline didn't get the best of them.

Garrett Hartley kept the Saints afloat with two first-half field goals of 46 and 44 yards, and he later added a 47-yarder to become the first kicker to make three from more than 40 yards in a Super Bowl.

That wasn't the greatest special teams moment, though.

SUPER SAINTS

149

31 **17**

The Saints' successfully pulled off an onside kick to start the second half, with safety Chris Reis recovering the ball.

SCOTT THRELKELD / THE TIMES-PICAYUNE

With New Orleans trailing 10-6, running back Pierre Thomas scores on a 16-yard touchdown pass to give the Saints their first lead.

ELIOT KAMENITZ / THE TIMES-PICAYUNE

SCOTT THRELKELD / THE TIMES-PICAYUNE
On a two-point conversion in the fourth quarter, receiver Lance Moore secures the ball to push New Orleans' lead to 24-17.

Coming out of halftime and trailing 10-6, Payton decided to dial up an onside kick. New Orleans had worked on it in practice over the last two weeks, but kicker Thomas Morstead was stunned when he was told they were putting it into action right before he took the field.

"I wasn't worried," Morstead said. "I was terrified."

He pulled it off, though, and safety Chris Reis and linebacker Jonathan Casillas were there for the recovery.

Six plays later, the Saints led 13-10 after a 16-yard screen pass from Brees to running back Pierre Thomas, aided by outstanding blocks by center Jonathan Goodwin and guard Jahri Evans.

After the game, Morstead found former NBA player/coach Avery Johnson in the locker room and thanked him for his words in a pregame motivational speech.

Johnson had told the players to play their role, to be themselves as they had all season, and that would be enough to win this game.

GAME STATISTICS
Attendance: 74,059 at Sun Life Stadium

TED JACKSON / THE TIMES PICAYUNE

Reggie
Bush

INDIVIDUAL STATISTICS

RUSHING
SAINTS: Pierre Thomas 9-30, Reggie Bush 5-25.
COLTS: Joseph Addai 13-77, Donald Brown 4-18.

PASSING
SAINTS: Drew Brees 32-39-288-2-0.
COLTS: Peyton Manning 31-45-333-1-1.

RECEIVING
SAINTS: Marques Colston 7-83, Devery Henderson 7-63.
COLTS: Dallas Clark 7-86, Joseph Addai 7-58.

INTERCEPTIONS
SAINTS: Tracy Porter 1.
COLTS: none.

SACKS
SAINTS: none.
COLTS: Dwight Freeney 1.

TACKLES (unassisted)
SAINTS: Jonathan Vilma 7, Roman Harper 6.
COLTS: Gary Brackett 12, Jacob Lacey 6.

SCORING SUMMARY

1ST
COLTS: Matt Stover 38-yard field goal. Eleven plays, 53 yards in 5:53.
COLTS: Pierre Garcon 19-yard pass from Peyton Manning (Stover kick). Eleven plays, 96 yards in 4:36.

2ND
SAINTS: Garrett Hartley 46-yard field goal. Eleven plays, 60 yards in 6:02.
SAINTS: Hartley 44-yard field goal. Five plays, 26 yards in 35 seconds.

3RD
SAINTS: Pierre Thomas 16-yard pass from Drew Brees (Hartley kick). Six plays, 58 yards in 3:19.
COLTS: Joseph Addai 4-yard run (Stover kick). Ten plays, 76 yards in 5:26.
SAINTS: Hartley 47-yard field goal. Eight plays, 37 yards in 4:14.

4TH
SAINTS: Jeremy Shockey 2-yard pass from Brees (two-point conversion successful). Nine plays, 59 yards in 4:57.
SAINTS: Tracy Porter 74-yard interception return (Hartley kick).

TEAM STATISTICS

	SAINTS	COLTS
FIRST DOWNS		
	20	23
TOTAL OFFENSIVE PLAYS-YARDS (NET)		
	58-332	64-432
RUSHES-YARDS (NET)		
	18-51	19-99
PASSING YARDS (NET)		
	281	333
PASSES (COMP-ATT-INT)		
	32-39-0	31-45-1
PUNTS (NUMBER-AVG)		
	2-44.0	2-45.0
PUNT RETURNS-YARDS		
	1-4	1-0
KICKOFF RETURNS-YARDS		
	4-102	5-111
PENALTY YARDS		
	3-19	5-45
FUMBLES-LOST		
	0-0	0-0
TIME OF POSSESSION		
	30:11	29:49
FIELD GOALS (ATT-MADE)		
	3-3	2-1

With the outcome hanging in the balance, the Saints get the better of quarterback Peyton Manning and Indianapolis.

Morstead said as a rookie it was important for him to remember that he just had to be himself in the game. Johnson, who told the team this summer to "Be Special," told them that they had made it through the letter A against Minnesota in a 31-28 overtime victory in the NFC championship game Jan. 24 at the Superdome when they had the right attitude and annihilated the quarterback.

Now it was time for the letter L to finish it off.

"He said if it's your job to be a leader, lead. If it's your job to make the guys laugh, do that," Shanle said. "Don't changed what you've done all year just because it's a big game.

"Hey, this team doesn't have more Pro Bowlers than everyone else in the league or more talent across the board. But nobody cares about each other more than we do."

Brees later talked about playing for a city and a region that rebuilt along with him after Hurricane Katrina, and he talked about a "Who Dat nation that has been behind us every step of the way."

When he finally was done talking to wave after wave of reporters, he went into a small room to remove his jersey and shoulder pads and share some hugs with the team equipment managers and another special "Who Dat" who was in attendance — former Saints linebacker Rickey Jackson, who one day earlier had become the first Pro Football Hall of Famer in the franchise's history.

Based on what he had accomplished over the past four years in New Orleans and what he did against the Colts, Brees was well on his way to joining him in with that select group of NFL greats in Canton, Ohio.

Quarterback Drew Bress marched the Saints to victory in Super Bowl XLIV, and in the process cemented his legend in New Orleans.

TED JACKSON / THE TIMES-PICAYUNE

Quarterback Drew Brees delivers in the clutch, and New Orleans is forever in his debt

JEFF DUNCAN

In New Orleans on Feb. 7, 2010, Rev. Msgr. Crosby W. Kern celebrated mass with a Drew Brees jersey underneath his vestments.

Later that night in Miami, Saints quarterback Drew Brees stood atop a gridiron alter and accepted the Pete Rozelle trophy as the MVP of Super Bowl XLIV after his near flawless performance against the Indianapolis Colts in New Orleans' 31-17 victory.

The citizens of New Orleans elected a new mayor — Mitch Landrieu — on Feb. 6, and they were set to crown a new king of Carnival on Feb. 16.

But New Orleans was forever in Brees' debt. He will never buy another drink, never purchase another meal and never pay another parking ticket.

It was forever his city. We just lived in it.

Brees etched his place in city legend alongside Bienville, Iberville and Armstrong with one of the great passing performances in Super Bowl history.

He completed 32 of 39 passes for 288 yard with two touchdowns in a masterpiece that vanquished the Colts and four-time league MVP Peyton Manning, a former standout at Isidore Newman School.

It also completed what Brees deemed "a calling" when he signed with the franchise as an unrestricted free agent only months after Hurricane Katrina devastated the city and region in 2005.

"This is incredible," Brees said. "I mean are you kidding, are you kidding me? Four years ago, whoever thought this would be happening? It's unbelievable."

Unbelievable was an accurate way to describe Brees' performance in the final three quarters against the Colts.

He had completed an uncharacteristic three of seven passes for 27 yards in the first quarter, but the rest of the way, he completed 29 of 32 passes for 261 yards, with two touchdowns and a two-point conversion.

Two of his incompletions were a spike to stop the clock and a dropped ball by running back Reggie Bush in the third quarter.

Brees saved his best for last.

With the game on the line, he engineered a drive that will stand the test of time for Who Dats.

With New Orleans trailing 17-16 with about 10 minutes remaining, he completed all seven of his passes for 40 yards in a nine-play, 59-yard scoring march. Each completion went to a different player.

They were in order:
► Running back Pierre Thomas for 5 yards.
► Receiver Devery Henderson for 6.
► Bush for 8.
► Receiver Marques Colston for 8.
► Receiver Robert Meachem for 6.
► Tight end David Thomas for 5.
► Tight end Jeremy Shockey for the final 2.

For good measure, Brees connected with receiver Lance Moore on a two-point conversion.

Eight pass attempts. Eight players making catches. None of the completions traveled more than 9 yards.

How was that for finishing strong?

"He was spectacular," Shockey said.

Said New Orleans guard Jahri Evans: "His performance was awesome. He's been awesome all year, and today he showed it."

Brees' heroics fueled a nearly perfect final three quarters of football from the Saints, who spotted the Colts a 10-0 lead, then stormed from behind as they had all season. His 32 completions tied the Super Bowl record set by Tom Brady of the New England Patriots against the Carolina Panthers in 2004.

On the same field where he directed one of the greatest comebacks in club history against the Miami Dolphins on Oct. 25, 2009, Brees guided the Saints to scores on five of their six series in the final three quarters. They were a failed goal-line play away from going six for six.

"He just led," Colston said. "I'm just so proud of that guy and just so happy to be just associated with greatness in that way."

The signature victory completed an impressive postseason hat track for Brees. In consecutive playoff games, he outdueled the Arizona Cardinals' Kurt Warner, the Minnesota Vikings' Brett Favre and finally Manning.

His numbers in those three contests were staggering: 72 completions in 102 attempts for 732 yards, eight touchdowns and zero interceptions. His passer efficiency rating was 117.0.

"Brees was magnificent tonight," New Orleans Coach Sean Payton said. "He played so well, so efficiently. He was fantastic. He was fantastic all year. He's just a winner. Everywhere he's been, he's won it — and now he's won it for us."

Payton might as well have spoken for all of the Who Dat Nation with those words.

2009 FLASHBACK

NFL FINAL REGULAR SEASON STANDINGS

NFC SOUTH

TEAM	W-L-T	PCT	PF	PA	HOME	ROAD	AFC	NFC	DIV
x-Saints	13-3	.813	510	341	6-2	7-1	9-3	4-0	4-2
Falcons	9-7	.563	363	325	6-2	3-5	6-6	3-1	3-3
Panthers	8-8	.500	315	308	5-3	3-5	8-4	0-4	4-2
Buccaneers	3-13	.188	244	400	1-7	2-6	3-9	0-4	1-5

NFC NORTH

TEAM	W-L-T	PCT	PF	PA	HOME	ROAD	AFC	NFC	DIV
x-Vikings	12-4	.750	470	312	8-0	4-4	9-3	3-1	5-1
y-Packers	11-5	.688	461	297	6-2	5-3	9-3	2-2	4-2
Bears	7-9	.438	327	375	5-3	2-6	5-7	2-2	3-3
Lions	2-14	.125	262	494	2-6	0-8	1-11	1-3	0-6

NFC EAST

TEAM	W-L-T	PCT	PF	PA	HOME	ROAD	AFC	NFC	DIV
x-Cowboys	11-5	.688	361	250	6-2	5-3	9-3	2-2	4-2
y-Eagles	11-5	.688	429	337	6-2	5-3	9-3	2-2	4-2
Giants	8-8	.500	402	427	4-4	4-4	6-6	2-2	4-2
Redskins	4-12	0 .250	266	336	3-5	1-7	2-10	2-2

NFC WEST

TEAM	W-L-T	PCT	PF	PA	HOME	ROAD	AFC	NFC	DIV
x-Cardinals	10-6	.625	375	325	4-4	6-2	8-4	2-2	4-2
49ers	8-8	.500	330	281	6-2	2-6	7-5	1-3	5-1
Seahawks	5-11	.313	280	390	4-4	1-7	4-8	1-3	3-3
Rams	1-15	.063	175	436	0-8	1-7	1-11	0-4	0-6

AFC SOUTH

TEAM	W-L-T	PCT	PF	PA	HOME	ROAD	AFC	NFC	DIV
x-Colts	14-2	.875	416	307	7-1	7-1	10-2	4-0	6-0
Texans	9-7	.563	388	333	4-4	5-3	6-6	3-1	1-5
Titans	8-8	.500	354	402	5-3	3-5	4-8	4-0	2-4
Jaguars	7-9	.438	290	380	5-3	2-6	6-6	1-3	3-3

AFC NORTH

TEAM	W-L-T	PCT	PF	PA	HOME	ROAD	AFC	NFC	DIV
x-Bengals	10-6	.625	305	291	6-2	4-4	7-5	3-1	6-0
y-Ravens	9-7	.563	391	261	6-2	3-5	7-5	2-2	3-3
Steelers	9-7	.563	368	324	6-2	3-5	6-6	3-1	2-4
Browns	5-11	.313	245	375	3-5	2-6	5-7	0-4	1-5

AFC EAST

TEAM	W-L-T	PCT	PF	PA	HOME	ROAD	AFC	NFC	DIV
x-Patriots	10-6	.625	427	285	8-0	2-6	7-5	3-1	4-2
y-Jets	9-7	.563	348	236	4-4	5-3	7-5	2-2	2-4
Dolphins	7-9	.438	360	390	4-4	3-5	5-7	2-2	4-2
Bills	6-10	.375	258	326	3-5	3-5	4-8	2-2	2-4

AFC WEST

TEAM	W-L-T	PCT	PF	PA	HOME	ROAD	AFC	NFC	DIV
x-Chargers	13-3	.813	454	320	6-2	7-1	9-3	4-0	5-1
Broncos	8-8	.500	326	324	4-4	4-4	6-6	2-2	3-3
Oakland	5-11	.313	197	379	2-6	3-5	4-8	1-3	2-4
Kansas City	4-12	.250	294	424	1-7	3-5	3-9	1-3	2-4

x-won division
y-secured playoff spot

RUSTY COSTANZA / THE TIMES-PICAYUNE

Saints players gave fans much to celebrate during the 2009 season, and Bourbon Street — as usual — was party central.

TEAM STATISTICS

	SAINTS	OPPONENTS
Total first downs	348	310
First downs (rushing-passing-by penalty)	115-215-18	111-175-24
Third-down conversions	88/197	82/216
Fourth-down conversions	6/15	11/24
Total offensive yards	6,461	5,724
Offense (plays-average yards)	1,032-6.3	1,044-5.5
Total rushing yards	2,106	1,955
Rushing (plays-average yards)	468-4.5	435-4.5
Total passing yards	4,355	3,769
Passing (comp-att-int-avg)	378-544-12-8.3	330-574-26-6.9
Sacks	35	20
Field goals	22/28	27/32
Touchdowns (rushing-passing-returns-defensive)	64 (37-21-34-1-8)	37 (19-15-1-2)
Time of possession	31:36	29:14
Turnover ratio	+11	

SAINTS INDIVIDUAL DEFENSIVE STATISTICS

PLAYER	G	SOLO	AST	TOTAL	SACK	INT
Jonathan Vilma	16	87	23	110	2.0	3
Roman Harper	16	85	18	103	1.5	0
Darren Sharper	14	51	20	71	0.5	9
Scott Shanle	14	57	12	69	0.0	2
Tracy Porter	12	49	9	58	0.0	4
Scott Fujita	11	43	15	58	1.0	0
Malcolm Jenkins	14	49	6	55	0.0	1
Will Smith	16	36	13	49	13.0	1
Charles Grant	16	31	13	44	5.5	0
Jabari Greer	9	40	3	43	0.0	2
Anthony Hargrove	16	32	10	42	5.0	0
Randall Gay	14	32	5	37	1.0	1
Sedrick Ellis	10	26	8	34	2.0	0
Remi Ayodele	15	18	12	30	1.5	1
Troy Evans	16	25	4	29	0.0	0
Pierson Prioleau	16	26	2	29	0.0	0
Marvin Mitchell	14	23	3	27	0.0	0
Jonathan Casillas	11	11	8	20	0.0	0
Jo-Lonn Dunbar	9	13	7	20	0.0	0
Chris Reis	15	14	3	17	0.0	1
DeMario Pressley	7	15	0	15	0.0	0
Courtney Roby	15	13	0	13	0.0	0
Bobby McCray	16	8	4	12	1.5	0
Mike McKenzie	5	8	3	11	0.0	1

PLAYER	G	SOLO	AST	TOTAL	SACK	INT
Leigh Torrence	5	9	1	10	0.5	0
Jeff Charleston	16	8	2	10	0.0	0
Usama Young	12	6	2	8	0.0	1
Lynell Hamilton	9	4	0	4	0.0	0
Chris McAlister	2	4	0	4	0.0	0
Mike Bell	13	2	1	3	0.0	0
Jahri Evans	16	3	0	3	0.0	0
Devery Henderson	16	3	0	3	0.0	0
Robert Meachem	16	2	0	2	0.0	0
Anthony Waters	3	2	0	2	0.0	0
Jason Kyle	16	1	0	2	0.0	0
Kendrick Clancy	2	1	1	2	0.0	0
Tory Humphrey	1	1	0	1	0.0	0
David Thomas	15	1	0	1	0.0	0
Marcus Mailei	2	1	0	1	0.0	0
Rodney Leisle	1	1	0	1	0.0	0
Thomas Morstead	16	1	0	1	0.0	0
Zach Strief	16	1	0	1	0.0	0
Pierre Thomas	14	1	0	1	0.0	0
Lance Moore	7	1	0	1	0.0	0
Jeremy Shockey	14	1	0	1	0.0	0
Marques Colston	16	1	0	1	0.0	0
Reggie Bush	14	1	0	1	0.0	0

SAINTS INDIVIDUAL OFFENSIVE STATISTICS

PASSING

PLAYER	G	COMP	ATT	YDS	TD	INT
Drew Brees	15	363	514	4,388	34	11
Mark Brunell	16	15	30	102	0	1

RUSHING

PLAYER	G	RUSH	YDS	Y/G	AVG	TD
Pierre Thomas	14	147	793	56.6	5.4	6
Mike Bell	13	172	654	50.3	3.8	5
Reggie Bush	14	70	390	27.9	5.6	5
Lynell Hamilton	9	35	125	13.9	3.6	2
Robert Meachem	16	6	82	5.1	13.7	0
Drew Brees	15	22	33	2.2	1.5	2
Heath Evans	6	5	16	2.7	3.2	1
Devery Henderson	16	4	13	0.8	3.3	0
Marques Colston	16	1	6	0.4	6.0	0
Kyle Eckel	7	2	6	0.9	3.0	0
Mark Brunell	16	4	-12	-0.8	-3.0	0

RECEIVING

PLAYER	G	REC	YDS	Y/G	AVG	TD
Marques Colston	16	70	1,074	67.1	15.3	9
Devery Henderson	16	51	804	50.3	15.8	2
Robert Meachem	16	45	722	45.1	16.0	9
Jeremy Shockey	14	48	569	40.6	11.9	3
David Thomas	15	35	356	23.7	10.2	1
Reggie Bush	14	47	335	23.9	7.1	3
Pierre Thomas	14	39	302	21.6	7.7	2
Lance Moore	7	14	153	21.9	10.9	2
Heath Evans	6	10	70	11.7	7.0	2
Lynell Hamilton	9	5	48	5.3	9.6	0
Darnell Dinkins	11	5	22	2.0	4.4	1
Kyle Eckel	7	2	14	2.0	7.0	0
Mike Bell	13	4	12	0.9	3.0	0
Tory Humphrey	1	1	7	7.0	7.0	0
Courtney Roby	15	1	6	0.4	6.0	0
Drew Brees	15	1	-4	-0.3	-4.0	0

FIELD GOALS AND EXTRA POINTS

PLAYER	G	FGM	FGA	LONG	XPM	XPA
John Carney	11	13	17	49	50	52
Garrett Hartley	5	9	11	58	10	11

KICKOFFS AND PUNT RETURNS

PLAYER	G	KR	TD	PR	LONG	TD
Courtney Roby	15	42	1	0	0	0
Robert Meachem	16	6	0	0	0	0
Mike Bell	13	2	0	0	0	0
Pierre Thomas	14	1	0	0	0	0
Lynell Hamilton	9	3	0	0	0	0
Jeff Charleston	16	2	0	0	0	0
Darnell Dinkins	11	1	0	0	0	0
Reggie Bush	14	0	0	27	23	0
Darren Sharper	14	0	0	1	6	0
Devery Henderson	16	0	0	4	11	0
Lance Moore	7	0	0	1	0	0

PUNTING

PLAYER	G	PUNT	AVG	IN20	IN10	TB
Thomas Morstead	16	58	43.6	18	11	4

SAINTS ROSTER

NO	PLAYER	POS	HT	WT	AGE	EXP	COLLEGE
87	Adrian Arrington	WR	6-3	192	24	2	Michigan
92	Remi Ayodele	DT	6-2	318	26	3	Oklahoma
21	Mike Bell	RB	6-0	225	26	4	Arizona
9	Drew Brees	QB	6-0	209	31	9	Purdue
11	Mark Brunell	QB	6-1	217	39	17	Washington
25	Reggie Bush	RB	6-0	203	24	4	Southern Cal
74	Jermon Bushrod	T	6-5	315	25	3	Towson
52	Jonathan Casillas	LB	6-1	227	22	R	Wisconsin
97	Jeff Charleston	DE	6-4	265	27	3	Idaho State
12	Marques Colston	WR	6-4	225	26	4	Hofstra
10	Chase Daniel	QB	6-0	225	23	R	Missouri
80	Darnell Dinkins	TE	6-4	260	33	8	Pittsburgh
36	Kyle Eckel	FB	5-11	237	28	3	Navy
98	Sedrick Ellis	DT	6-1	307	24	2	Southern Cal
54	Troy Evans	LB	6-3	238	32	8	Cincinnati
73	Jahri Evans	G	6-4	318	26	4	Bloomsburg
55	Scott Fujita	LB	6-5	250	30	8	California
20	Randall Gay	CB	5-11	190	27	6	LSU
76	Jonathan Goodwin	C	6-3	318	31	8	Michigan
32	Jabari Greer	CB	5-11	180	27	6	Tennessee
30	Lynell Hamilton	RB	6-0	235	24	1	San Diego St.
69	Anthony Hargrove	DL	6-3	272	26	5	Georgia Tech
41	Roman Harper	S	6-1	200	27	4	Alabama
5	Garrett Hartley	K	5-8	196	23	2	Oklahoma
19	Devery Henderson	WR	5-11	200	27	6	LSU
84	Tory Humphrey	TE	6-2	255	27	4	Central Mich.
27	Malcolm Jenkins	CB	6-0	204	22	R	Ohio State
57	Jason Kyle	LS	6-3	242	37	15	Arizona State
60	Nick Leckey	C	6-3	291	27	6	Kansas State
93	Bobby McCray	DE	6-6	260	28	6	Florida
17	Robert Meachem	WR	6-2	210	25	3	Tennessee
50	Marvin Mitchell	LB	6-3	249	25	3	Tennessee
16	Lance Moore	WR	5-9	190	26	4	Toledo
6	Thomas Morstead	P	6-4	225	23	R	S. Methodist
67	Jamar Nesbit	G	6-4	328	33	11	South Carolina
77	Carl Nicks	G/T	6-5	343	24	2	Nebraska
22	Tracy Porter	CB	5-11	186	23	2	Indiana
90	DeMario Pressley	DT	6-3	301	24	2	N. C. State
31	Pierson Prioleau	S	5-11	188	32	11	Virginia Tech
39	Chris Reis	S	6-1	215	26	3	Georgia Tech
15	Courtney Roby	WR	6-0	189	27	4	Indiana
58	Scott Shanle	LB	6-2	245	30	7	Nebraska
42	Darren Sharper	S	6-2	210	34	13	William & Mary
88	Jeremy Shockey	TE	6-5	251	29	8	Miami
91	Will Smith	DE	6-3	282	28	6	Ohio State
96	Paul Spicer	DE	6-4	295	34	10	Saginaw Valley St.
78	Jon Stinchcomb	T	6-5	315	30	7	Georgia
64	Zach Strief	T	6-7	320	26	4	Northwestern
23	Pierre Thomas	RB	5-11	215	25	3	Illinois
85	David Thomas	TE	6-3	248	26	4	Texas
51	Jonathan Vilma	LB	6-1	230	27	6	Miami
59	Anthony Waters	LB	6-3	238	25	3	Clemson
28	Usama Young	S	6-0	200	24	3	Kent State

2009 SAINTS DRAFT PICKS (April 25-26)

ROUND	OVERALL PICK	PLAYER	POSITION	HT	WT	SCHOOL
1	14	Malcolm Jenkins	CB	6-0	204	Ohio State
4	116	Chip Vaughn	S	6-2	221	Wake Forest
4	*118	Stanley Arnoux	LB	6-0	232	Wake Forest
5	**164	Thomas Morstead	P	6-4	225	Southern Methodist

*From the New York Jets
**From the New York Giants through the Philadelphia Eagles

CHUCK COOK / THE TIMES-PICAYUNE

SUPER SAINTS

2009 RECORDS

SAINTS TEAM RECORDS SET DURING THE 2009 REGULAR SEASON

510 Most points

64 Most touchdowns

7 Most touchdowns in a game, (tied) vs. Giants on Oct. 18

34 Most passing touchdowns, (tied)

6 Most passing touchdowns in a game, (tied) vs. Lions on Sept. 13

13 Longest winning streak, (games 1-13)

9.6 Highest average yards per play in a game, vs. Patriots on Nov. 30

652 Most interception return yards

5 Most interceptions returned for touchdowns, (tied)

2 Most interceptions returned for touchdowns in a game, at Dolphins on Sept. 25

SAINTS INDIVIDUAL RECORDS SET DURING THE 2009 REGULAR SEASON

COMPLETION PERCENTAGE: *70.62, Drew Brees
PASSER RATING: 109.6, Brees
PASSER RATING IN A GAME: *158.3, Brees vs. Patriots on Nov. 30
TOUCHDOWN PASSES: 34 (tied), Brees
TOUCHDOWN PASSES IN A GAME: six (tied), Brees vs. Lions on Sept. 13
TOUCHDOWN PASSES (CAREER): 122, Brees

MOST CONSECUTIVE COMPLETIONS: 19, Brees vs. Buccaneers on Dec. 27
MOST INTERCEPTION RETURN YARDAGE: *376, Darren Sharper
MOST INTERCEPTIONS RETURNED FOR TOUCHDOWNS: three, Sharper
LONGEST INTERCEPTION RETURN FOR A TOUCHDOWN: 99 yards, Sharper vs. the Jets on Oct. 4

*set or tied NFL record

2009 INDIVIDUAL HONORS

QUARTERBACK DREW BREES
The Sporting News' Offensive Player of the Year
Pro Bowl selection
FedEx Air Player of the Week (weeks 1, 2, 6, 12 and 14)
FedEx Air Player of the Year
The Associated Press NFL All-Pro team (second team)

GUARD JAHRI EVANS
The Associated Press NFL All-Pro team (first team)
Pro Bowl selection
CENTER JONATHAN GOODWIN
Pro Bowl selection
SAFETY ROMAN HARPER
Pro Bowl selection

SAFETY DARREN SHAPER
The Associated Press NFL All-Pro team (first team), Pro Bowl selection
TACKLE JON STINCHCOMB
Pro Bowl selection
LINEBACKER JONATHAN VILMA
Pro Bowl selection
COACH SEAN PAYTON
The Sporting News' Coach of the Year

THE ROAD TO SUPER BOWL XLIV

WILD-CARD ROUND	DIVISIONAL ROUND	NFC CHAMPIONSHIP	SUPER BOWL XLIV	AFC CHAMPIONSHIP	DIVISIONAL ROUND	WILD-CARD ROUND

Final in overtime — Cardinals 51 (4)
Packers 45 (5)

Final — Saints 45 (1)
Cardinals 14

Final in overtime — Saints 31

Final — Cowboys 34 (3)
Eagles 14 (6)

Final — Vikings 34 (2)
Cowboys 3

Vikings 28

Colts 30

Jets 17

Final — Colts 20 (1)
Ravens 3

Final — Chargers 14 (2)
Jets 17

Final — Patriots 14 (3)
Ravens 33 (6)

Final — Bengals 14 (4)
Jets 24 (5)

Note: Highest seeded team had home-field advantage; ● = seed

THE TIMES-PICAYUNE

BLAST FROM THE PAST

SAINTS YEARLY RETURNS

2009
13-3-0
Sean Payton

2008
8-8-0
Sean Payton

2007
7-9-0
Sean Payton

2006
10-6-0
Sean Payton

2005
3-13-0
Jim Haslett

2004
8-8-0
Jim Haslett

2003
8-8-0
Jim Haslett

2002
9-7-0
Jim Haslett

2001
7-9-0
Jim Haslett

2000
10-6-0
Jim Haslett

1999
3-13-0
Mike Ditka

1998
6-10-0
Mike Ditka

1997
6-10-0
Mike Ditka

1996
3-13-0
Jim Mora

1995
7-9-0
Jim Mora

1994
7-9-0
Jim Mora

1993
8-8-0
Jim Mora

1992
12-4-0
Jim Mora

1991
11-5-0
Jim Mora

1990
8-8-0
Jim Mora

1989
9-7-0
Jim Mora

1988
10-6-0
Jim Mora

1987
12-3-0
Jim Mora

1986
7-9-0
Jim Mora

1985
5-11-0
Bum Phillips (4-8-0)
Wade Phillips (1-3-0)

1984
7-9-0
Bum Phillips

1983
8-8-0
Bum Phillips

1982
4-5-0
Bum Phillips

1981
4-12-0
Bum Phillips

1980
1-15-0
Dick Nolan (0-12),
Dick Stanfel (1-3)

1979
8-8-0
Dick Nolan

1978
7-9-0
Dick Nolan

1977
3-11-0
Hank Stram

1976
4-10-0
Hank Stram

1975
2-12-0
John North (1-5-0),
Ernie Hefferle (1-7-0)

1974
5-9-0
John North

1973
5-9-0
John North

1972
2-11-1
J.D. Roberts

1971
4-8-2
J.D. Roberts

1970
2-11-1
Tom Fears (1-5-1),
J.D. Roberts (1-6-0)

1969
5-9-0
Tom Fears

1968
4-9-1
Tom Fears

1967
3-11-0
Tom Fears

RETIRED NUMBERS BY THE SAINTS

31
JIM TAYLOR
(but assigned to active players)

81
DOUG ATKINS
(but assigned to active players)

57
RICKEY JACKSON
(but assigned to active players)

8 Note: The No. 8 is not retired but has not been issued to any New Orleans player since quarterback Archie Manning was traded to the Houston Oilers in September 1982.

INDIVIDUALS THAT HAVE PLAYED/COACHED FOR THE SAINTS THAT ARE ENSHRINED AT THE PRO FOOTBALL HALL OF FAME IN CANTON, OHIO

INDIVIDUAL	POSITION	YEARS IN N.O.
Earl Campbell	Running back	1984-85
Jim Finks	General manager	1986-93
Hank Stram	Coach	1976-1977
Jim Taylor	Fullback	1967
Mike Ditka	Coach	1997-99
Tom Fears	Coach	1967-70

SAINTS HALL OF FAME

YEAR	PLAYER	POSITION
2009	Morten Andersen	Kicker
2008	Willie Roaf	Tackle
2007	Joe Johnson	Defensive end
*2005-2006	Joel Hilgenberg	Center
2004	Rueben Mayes	Running back
2004	Steve Sidwell	Assistant coach
2003	Wayne Martin	Defensive end
2003	Jim Dombrowski	Guard/tackle
2002	Jim Mora	Coach
2002	Frank Warren	Defensive end
2001	Hoby Brenner	Tight end
2001	Jim Wilks	Defensive end
2000	Vaughan Johnson	Linebacker
2000	Pat Swilling	Linebacker
1999	Bobby Hebert	Quarterback
1999	Eric Martin	Wide receiver
1998	Dalton Hilliard	Running back
1998	Sam Mills	Linebacker
1997	Rickey Jackson	Linebacker
1997	Stan Brock	Tackle
1996	Dave Whitsell	Cornerback
1996	Dave Waymer	Defensive back
1995	Bob Pollard	Defensive end
1995	Doug Atkins	Defensive end
1994	Jim Finks	General manager
1994	Henry Childs	Tight end
1993	Joe Federspiel	Linebacker
1992	George Rogers	Running back
1992	Jake Kupp	Guard
1992	John Hill	Center
1991	Derland Moore	Nose tackle
1991	Tony Galbreath	Running back
1990	Billy Kilmer	Quarterback
1989	Tommy Myers	Safety
1989	Tom Dempsey	Kicker
1988	Archie Manning	Quarterback
1988	Danny Abramowicz	Wide receiver

*2005 induction ceremonies postponed to Oct. 27, 2006, due to Hurricane Katrina.